A BETTER LOOK AT INTELLIGENT BEHAVIOR: COGNITION AND EMOTION

A BETTER LOOK AT INTELLIGENT BEHAVIOR: COGNITION AND EMOTION

FREDERIC PEREZ-ALVAREZ
AND
CARME TIMONEDA-GALLART

Nova Science Publishers, Inc.
New York

LIBRARY OF CONGRESS CATALOGING-IN-PUBLICATION DATA

Perez-Alvarez, Frederic.
A Better look at intelligent havior : cognition and emotion / Frederic Perez-Alvarez, Carme Timoneda-Gallart.
     p.cm
ISBN-13: 978-1-60021-742-5 (hardcover)
ISBN-10: 1-60021-742-7 (hardcover)
1. Emotions and cognition. 2. Cognition in children. 3. Emotions in children. 4. Child psychology.
I. Timoneda-Gallart, Carme. II. Title.
BF311.P3645   2007
155.4'18-dc22   2007016323

Published by Nova Science Publishers, Inc. ✦ *New York*

CONTENTS

Chapter 1

INTRODUCTION: METHODOLOGICAL FRAMEWORK

Since 1994, our research has been focussed on both normal children and non-normal children. So children with dislexia as well as learning problems in general [Perez-Alvarez & Timoneda, 1999d, 1999e, 2000, 2004a; Das et al. 2000], children suffering from attention deficit hyperactive disorder [Perez-Alvarez & Timoneda, 1999c, 1999d, 2001, 2004a, 2004b] and epilepsy [Perez-Alvarez & Timoneda, 1996; Perez-Alvarez et al.2002; Pérez-Álvarez et al, 2006a] have been the preferred focus of our published research. On the other hand, among our unpublished results, gifted children, those with autism and other developmental disorders, children with Down syndrome, Klinefelter syndrome, Williams syndrome [Perez-Alvarez et al. 1999] and other chromosomal anomalies, as well as children with encephalic lesion due to cranial traumatism, and neurofibromatosis among heredodegenerative diseases have been all studied by us. Furthermore, we have diagnosed and treated children with different kinds of behavioral problems [Perez-Alvarez & Timoneda, 1999a, 1999b, 2002].

Our research is based on both quantitative and qualitative investigation methods. Within the quantitative methods, the multivariate analysis as principal component factorial analysis with a maximum likelihood method of extraction and VARIMAX rotation was used, for instance, to validate the PASS (Planning, Attention, Simultaneous, Successive) cognitive DN:CAS (Das Naglieri Cognitive Assessment System) battery. Apart from generalized tests widely used for assessing differences between both means and proportions, as well as for assessing correlations, cluster analysis proved to be a particularly useful tool.

The qualitative investigation method [Jones, 1995; Mays & Pope, 1995, Greenhalgh & Taylor, 1997; Green & Britten, 1998; Crabtree & Miller, 1992; Creswell, 1994] was the only one possible, we think, to study the behavioral analysis based on our theoretical framework that makes "rating scales" useless, for instance, the "Child Behavior Rating Scale of Achenbach" or the "Facial Action Coding System" or the "Differential Emotional Scale". This method has been applied to a non-probabilistic sample (N = 1333), aged 5 – 15, recruited from patients pertaining to the normal socioeconomic community that usually uses our center, during the period January 1994 – December 2003 [Perez-Alvarez, 1999a, 1999b, 2002]. Our center is open to any kind of demand independent of the nature of the problem, benign or non-benign. Being diagnosed as suffering from any non-organic "disease" was the inclusion criterion. Different symptoms were initially reported, for instance, "having sleeping trouble", "feeling unhappy or sad", "having a headache or stomachache", "wetting the bed", "eating without appetite", or, simply, behavioral conflict at home and/or at school or poor academic performance and so on. Exhaustive medical investigation was done as needed. The diagnose-intervention procedure [Perez-Alvarez, 1999a, 1999b, 2002; Perez-Alvarez & Timoneda, 1998; Mayoral-Rodríguez, 2002; Alabau-Bofill, 2003] was carried out by the same professional for each case. We think that the sample of the population is large enough to deduce valid conclusions.

Medical checking was always carried out in order to rule out any pathological condition or frank neurological or psychiatric disorder. The protocol carried out included interviews of the child and his/her parents, interviews of his/her teacher and tutor, inquiry on his/her background from his/her regular doctor, detailed clinical anamnesis and exploration with attention to both general and neurological conditions, as well as ophthalmologic and otorhinolaryngologic condition. Any subject given any medication was excluded. Also, either personal or phone contact with the family doctor as well as contact with other professionals potentially working in parallel on the case were systematically carried out.

Qualitative data are both the verbal-linguistic behavior and the body-gesture language. From this point of view, behaviors are what we say and/or do as reading (straying onto lines above and below the one he/she is reading, for instance), speaking, learning. Likewise, being interested in, attentive or inattentive attitude, being motivated, a smiling unconcerned attitude, face puzzled on hearing something or seeing something, showing hesitation, interest, effort, enthusiasm, anxious behavior, uncertainty, yawning, face of indifference, of affliction, depressing face, happy face, discomfort with affectionate aggression, doing things at a hurried pace, answering impulsively, hysterical quality in the voice, calm tone of the voice, loudness of voice, nodding movement to express agreement or disagreement or understanding, looking away when uncomfortable and so forth. Body language allows us not only, and first of all, to assess feelings like happiness, affliction, anger and so on, but also to interpret the cognitive mental processing of ideas or concepts. So, in particular, the eye position allows us to know if simultaneous processing is working and the eye scanning tells us if planning is working. Likewise, a repeated verbal or sub - vocal rehearsal to facilitate recalling tells us the successive is working. Counting on his/her fingers may tell us mental counting is difficult.

Data ("dependent variables") are obtained from the patient or subject, the family, the teachers and any other members in inter-relationship with the case. Likewise, the data involving both linguistic and body language are clearly defined and collected via audio-video recording, implying an observation-registration process to get the utmost accuracy. Also, data are spontaneously collected without directive intervention to avoid the bias derived from the personal beliefs of the interviewer who follows a non-structured interview-like system. It is about an external observational procedure without direct participation, the researcher not being part of the observed universe.

The raw observed and collected data allow the investigator to interpret the beliefs linked to the bad feeling forming part of the memorized information (cognitive beliefs + feeling) that constitutes the personal identity, that is, self - concept, self – esteem, self – confidence in psychological terms. The "independent variable" is the normalized procedure of diagnosis – intervention clearly defined and previously published [Perez-Alvarez & Timoneda, 1998; Mayoral-Rodríguez, 2002; Alabau-Bofill, 2003]. Usually, 1 hour sessions, 1 per week, during 3 to 6 months was carried out. Diagnosis and Treatment work together since the beginning, the therapeutic effect consisting of making the person change the memorized painful feeling linked to personal cognitive beliefs to such an extent as to decrease the threshold of triggering in the cerebral temporal amygdala, according to the most recent neurological evidence.

Treatment is based on communication techniques focussed on getting a change of beliefs (from destructive to constructive beliefs) and associated feelings, with the always present aim of avoiding the non-constructive response to painful feeling processing in learning and behavior.

The instrument for "measuring" or assessing the data is the observer-investigator. His/her judgement, making inferences, is the instrument for interpreting the data. To control and avoid the inaccuracy (bias) characteristic of the intra-observer variability that produces subjective individual error, a triangulation technique that produces the so-called "alien independent investigator effect" was carried out systematically. On purpose, every case was discussed in clinical session and inter – investigator agreement of 80% on any controversial question was needed.

To minimize the so-called "effect of the observer on the observed", each case was carried out by the same professional from the beginning to the end. The confounding effect and subsequent bias attributable to the empathic effect must be considered controlled, as far as possible, taking into account that the procedure [Perez-Alvarez & Timoneda, 1998; Mayoral-Rodríguez, 2002; Alabau-Bofill, 2003] implies empathic communication, but not sympathetic identification. As a further control to the bias arising from the observed-observer interaction, it must be emphasized that even though the observed subject knows he/she is observed and he/she could introduce the confounding effect of not being willing, however the involuntary masked painful emotional behaviors are involuntarily triggered, not susceptible therefore to be avoided by the will.

A very important methodological point is defining the criterion of success of the procedure in the sense we assume that the procedure is successful because it is able to eliminate the reactive painful emotional behaviors to a extent that it means that the cerebral memorization of pain linked to memorized personal beliefs has changed enough to make it unnecessary to be reacting with masked painful-emotional behaviors to the same degree as before. So the success was defined as not only the disappearance of the dysfunctional behavior causing the demand, but also the disappearance to a sufficient extent of the profuse associated masked painful-emotional behaviors. The reduction of, at least, 50% of the set of masked painful emotional behaviors, which was linked to a more satisfactory life was considered "enough" improvement. To measure this last condition, the investigator contrasted it with the fathers, the other family members, the friends, the teachers, and so on. A follow-up consisting of yearly phone contact was carried out, being successful in 54 % of cases on the average.

Since 1998, all the cases (n = 703), independent of his/her nature, whether cognitive or non-cognitive, are administered the translated and validated PASS cognitive battery DN:CAS [Naglieri & Das, 1997] in order to know the particular cognitive functioning. Later, we would see its diagnostic utility even in diagnosing emotional dysfunctional behavior.

Concerning qualitative research, the method explained is subject to the limitations of qualitative investigations, but it meets sufficient criteria of both validity and reliability to guarantee results and conclusions excluding the chance or placebo effect. On the other hand, we must remember that quantitative research is not free of limitations [Ionnidis, 2005].

Regarding methodological aspects, finally, we have made a magnetic resonance image (fMRI) study [Perez-Alvarez et al. 2006b] consisting of investigating the fMRI pattern in 15 subjects as they make decisions on painful feeling dilemmas [Greene et al. 2001] in comparison with non-painful feeling dilemmas. The aim was to identify neurological areas involved in decision-making (planning), when painful feeling processing is involved. A new fMRI study focussed on attention deficit hyperactive disorder (ADHD) is being carried out by our group. From a previous report on ADHD and positron emission tomography (PET) profiles [Amen & Carmichael, 1997], we have designed a study oriented to identify fMRI profiles in ADHD children by using the tasks we utilized for our study on decision making [Perez-Alvarez et al.,2006b] as a discriminating test between ADHD children and normal control ones.

At this point, some comments on casualty are needed [Balmes,1968; Shand, 2000]. The act of reasoning consists of thoughts that are causal processes. Scientifically speaking, the aim of any study on behavior is to discover the cause of the behavior. In defining any cause we must keep in mind that a cause is followed by a consequence. In other words a cause is something that determines something else as a necessary and sufficient condition or, if multiple conditions are involved, as each necessary and jointly sufficient condition.

Anyway, our aim must be to identify the first cause in a chain of causes, and, on the other hand, to differentiate a precipitant non-necessary non-sufficient causal factor from an essential necessary sufficient factor. What is not necessary is in fact contingent (could have been otherwise). Strikingly, we can hear or read that a child does not learn because he/she is not interested in, motivated, does not pay attention, and does not make an effort. Frequently, this child is suffering from some cognitive difficulty or/and emotional disturbance as a first cause determining as a consequence lack of interest, motivation, paying attention and so on. This diagnosis is very crucial in order to plan a successful intervention.

Chapter 2

NEUROBIOLOGICAL CONCEPT OF BEHAVIOR

Behavior must be neuro-biologically considered any external manifestation of human beings whatsoever. In this sense, walking, eating, coughing, reading, writing, oppositional defiant behavior, but also learning and speaking, for instance, must be all considered behaviors [Delgado et al. 1998; Pinel, 2000]. Any behavior in action must be considered the consequence of two mental-neurological activities [Churland 1989]. One, the cognitive activity and the other, the feeling-sensitivity activity.

The previous examples of behavior meet the criterion of being the response (output) component in the information processing mechanism (Das, 1999; Das et al. 1994, 1996, 2000). The central processing of information happens between the information entering via sensorial input, whether visual, auditory or kinesthetic, and either verbal or non-verbal output. Input, central processing and output can occur either consciously or unconsciously. This principle of functioning is true for both physical somatic-visceral information and both cognitive information or feeling-emotional-sensitivity. This conception proves to be essential to understand how the personal beliefs mentally-neurologically work (Bateson, 1979).

We mean that whenever a behavior is occurring, the central nervous system (CNS) is processing a cognitive-data content, either consciously or unconsciously, and the feeling-sensitivity associated with the cognitive content, also either consciously or unconsciously. Both the cognitive component and the feeling-sensitivity component form part of the experienced-memorized knowledge we call beliefs. We claim that the sensitive component of the belief, but not the cognitive component, is the determinant causal factor of the behaviors (Power, & Dalgleish, 1997).

Keeping in mind these concepts, we will illustrate how the behaviors (Bateson, 1979) can be explained according to the cognitive processing (Das, 1999; Das et al., 1994, 1996, 2000; Perez-Alvarez & Timoneda, 2004) and the painful feeling processing (LeDoux, 1995, 1996, 2000; LeDoux et al., 1984, 1986, 1990; Damasio, 1994, 1995, 1999; Power & Dalgleish, 1997; Goldberg, 2001; Greene et al., 2001; Singer et al., 2004; Camille et al., 2004; Bechara, 2004), the emphasis being put on the neurological processing foundation.

Strictly speaking, behavior (Bateson, 1979) must be considered anything an organism does, that is, any observable activity directly correlated with mental-psychic activity supported by neurological networks. Communication in network is obliged when the magnitude of interchangeable information of a neuron makes it necessary. Note that a motor-neuron connect with 3000 to 5000 interneurons to interchange information. Mental activity happens while the neurological networks are working. Knowing how the neurological networks operate, we can better understand how mental activity takes place. As we have said, therefore, behaviors are motion, speaking, learning, crying, aggression, and so on. At least two mental processes are operating whenever a behavior is put into action, the cognitive processing of information and the feeling processing and, in particular, painful feeling processing.

Cognitive functioning has not yet been unequivocally defined. The heterogeneity in results reported so far is again and again argued to be due to methodological difficulties. However, the first difficulty to solve is to define what cognitive function is about. For instance, learning difficulties are different in nature depending on whether they are due to tremor because of cerebellar dysfunction (somatic neuronal network), or due to exact failure in mental cognitive processing (cognitive neuronal network) or, may be, failure in social affective adjustment (feeling neuronal network). So academic failure can be due to cognitive failure, but also to emotional-affective disturbances and even to a physical somatic-visceral disorder or a sum of all these factors. The cognition concept deserves an appropriate clarification. We claim the cognitive function term refers to the scientifically validated mental-neurological function supported by a neurological network, whether known or supposed.

The evidence we count on tells us that the central nervous system works in circuitry terms similarly regardless of the somatic-visceral or cognitive-emotional nature of the network. So it is reasonable to assume that what we know about a kind of network is susceptible to be applied to the other network. Both cognitive - emotional and somatic - visceral neurons share anatomy and physiology, that is, projection and intercalary neurons, astrocytes, oligodendrocytes, microglia, physiologic properties, neurotransmitters receptors [Olpe & Schellenberg, 1981], ionic channels, action potential, signal transmission, and so on.

Regarding neurotransmitters, for instance, we can comment that acetylcholine has been linked to paying attention, learning and memory; norepinephrine - adrenaline to arousal and spirits; dopamine to arousal and motor functions; serotonin to spirits; and glutamate to learning and long-term memory. Some neurological areas have been identified to be particularly rich in a concrete neurotransmitter. For instance, the inferior fronto - temporal area is rich in GABA, basal nuclei of the brain in dopamine, raphe of brain stem in serotonin, locus coeruleus of brain stem in noradrenaline. However, the non-specificity of neurotransmitters [Delini-Stula & Schiwy, 1991] is such that we count on recent evidence that the dopamine receptor is able to transport serotonin when the serotonin receptor is saturated and serotonin is overflowing [Fu-Ming Zhou et al. 2005]. All point to the fact that what differentiates a somatic-visceral from an either cognitive or feeling neuron has to do with molecular (DNA / RNA) activity in the cell.

The non-specificity principle rules many neurological mechanisms. We can affirm that, in general, the neurophysiological mechanisms are not specific. For instance, we call a tranquilizer any agent that brings about a state of peace of mind or relief from anxiety. They produce a calming or sedative effect without inducing sleep. Some of them, classically called major tranquilizers like chlorpromazine and meprobamate, have antipsychotic effect. Others, called minor tranquilizers like diazepam, have no antipsychotic effect. However, any tranquilizer can produce a hypnotic effect (sleeping effect) depending on the doses and the idiosyncratic effect, a peculiarity of constitution that makes an individual react differently from most persons to drugs, diet, treatments, or other situations. Most important, as we will explain in another section, physical and psychological pain share the same neurological structures, and likewise the same physiological reaction to both physical and psychological pain happens by means of ACTH and endorphins.

From the point of view of assessment, any test by itself can be considered useful on a psychometric basis if it allows us to diagnose, for instance, a neurological disease, which is characteristic of clinical neuropsychology. In this case, the test is a useful measure as part of the signs and symptoms of the disease and nothing else is intended. For instance, in some way, it is similar to a sphygmodynamometer, an instrument for measuring the force of the pulse. From the point of view of cognitive etiopathogenesis, instead, the test being used not only must be conveniently validated but also validated in the sense of scientifically demonstrating that the results obtained convey the central neurological functioning, but not simply the result as signs and symptoms of something unknown. Etiopathogenic diagnosis is an advantage on a treatment basis. This conception is satisfied by the PASS theory of cognitive processing of information [Das et al. 1979, 1994, 1996, 1999a; Timoneda & Perez-Alvarez, 1994].

What a test assesses depends on the concepts it is based on, which determines how it is constructed. Traditionally, a test has been constructed on the basis of knowing from observation that any human being is able to perform something (ability), then the test is standardized and the percentage limits of normality are defined. Everybody assumes that there is a mental process behind the resolution capacity. According to this, what is measured (the resulting score) is a behavior produced by a particular human being that time and that day. In fact, this is equivalent to measuring any other corporal behavior like, for instance, motion capacity. We can create a test to score the performance in a concrete movement capacity. The DN:CAS battery [Das & Naglieri, 1997] for assessing the PASS processing measures a resulting behavior in a test, but also tells us, by knowing the results in all the tests (quantitative assessment) and how the tests are performed (qualitative assessment), that a particular bad result in a concrete test of the battery can be changed for the better if the inefficient mental operation now applied is later applied in another different way either spontaneously or by tutored training. This implies a dynamic concept of intelligent behavior. This mental operational changing can be facilitated by a suitable remediation program [Das, 1999b]. In other words, the DN:CAS gives us a profile that is non-static but dynamic, that is, changeable.

This battery informs us how efficiently four identified mental cognitive programs work, namely, Planning, Attention, Simultaneous, and Successive (PASS). Taking into account the conception, a clear distinction must be immediately established between attentive behavior and attention cognitive processing, between sequential behavior and successive cognitive processing, between simultaneous behavior and simultaneous cognitive processing, and between planned behavior and planning as cognitive processing. These four programs are always working whenever any cognitive activity takes place independently of how an information is either entering (input) or leaving (output) the central nervous system (CNS). In fact, this is not different from what the CNS does with any kind of information being processed. For instance, ataxia must be considered a resulting behavior that can be due to failure in the cerebellar neuronal network (program), but also in the vestibular neuronal network (program). The same output can be due to different central programs. Also, something not different from the fact that different sums (programs) can actually produce the same sum (output) like $3+3$, $4+2$, $1+5 = 6$. The same result, but different programs.

The four PASS programs were identified by considering how the CNS processes the cognitive information according to the Luria's studies of lesions [Luria,1980; Das, 1999a]. This implies a different theoretical framework as we will see later on. In essence, the basic conclusion consisted of observing that the same neurons produced different results (signs and symptoms) and vice versa, that is, different neurons produced the same result.

Arising from this, concrete tests were created first and then factor analysis validated by comparing PASS tests with non-PASS tests known earlier. This way, we have got to know the non-verbal tests of K-ABC, Wechsler, Binet 4, and McCarthy assess PASS simultaneous and something else non-equivalent to PASS processing, while the tests of these previously mentioned batteries measure some PASS processing and sometimes something else non-comparable to. Likewise, the Forward Span assess PASS successive, while the Backward Span measures PASS successive and planning. In addition, the Wisconsin test measures PASS planning, but also something else non-PASS. And, the Stroop test measures PASS attention. This process led to isolating the tests specifically measuring each of the four PASS processes [Das et al. 1994]. We will return to this theme conveniently.

Within these preliminary ideas, we will begin with a brief discussion of PASS. The PASS concept can be exemplified as follows: to remember the input 633435, you may do it by recalling the series with no other association (relationship) but only the lineal association, one digit after the following. Something like rote memorization of the kind of subvocal rehearsal for recalling a series, for instance. If so, you are operating with successive processing that works whenever working memory (Baddeley & Hitch, 1974) is operating. A fMRI model of working memory, which assigns ventro-lateral prefrontal (BA 45, 47) to short memory and dorso-lateral prefrontal (BA 9, 46) to executive function, has been described [Petrides, 1994]. Also another fMRI model [Van den Heuvel, 2005] has been recently reported. According to this model, a fronto-striatal system is defined, but what matters is they distinguish three prefrontal lobes. One is the dorso-lateral prefrontal cortex (DLPFC) with Brodmann areas (BA) 9 and 46. Second is the ventro-lateral perfrontal cortex (VLPFC) with BAs 44, 45 and 47. Third is the anterior prefrontal cortex (APFC) with BAs 8 and 10. They consider that the DLPFC and VLPFC form working memory, which means that the non-lateral prefrontal is not exactly linked to cognitive function. They also set up lateral prefrontal together with posterior brain, namely, parietal and occipital form a network linked to conscious cognitive processing. They relate all these structures to their concept of planning because the tasks they used demand planning but also successive and simultaneous in PASS terms. We think the PASS concept is a more accurate conceptualization.

Instead, you can do it by recalling it as 63 34 35, in which case you are using the successive processing for recording three units, that is, 63 / 34 / 35, but each unit has been mentally elaborated with simultaneous processing, which allows us to establish the relationship $6 + 3 = 63$. The simultaneous also works whenever working memory works, but it is more relevant for long-term-memory. On the other hand, you can think as previously mentioned, but, also, you can think 63 / 34 / 35 is as if 34, 35 and 36 in consecutive order, but turning 36 into 63 and translating the last unit to the first one in the series. In such a case planning allows you to operate with this mental strategy. Attention processing is always present and it is different from attention behavior. For example, inattentive behavior involves the attention processing when mental activity is focussed on another someone / something.

This concept means that the same individual can resolve the problem of the sequence presented, now using his/her bad successive, unsuccessfully (bad result = low intelligence?), but, just hours later, using his/her good simultaneous, successfully (good result = high intelligence?). Similarly, an inattentive child (description of the behavior observed) can be an excellent PASS attentive processor, when we assess the PASS mental operation of being attentive. Or a disorganized child (description for an unplanned observed behavior) can be a very good PASS mental planner. In this line, knowing either a negative result in a test or the negative effect of a drug on a particular memory test, for instance, is not so relevant as knowing the resulting performance was due to the use of an inefficient PASS program that can be left out and substituted for another more efficient PASS program in order to achieve a better result.

In advance, we'll say that the PASS processing programs can be related to particular regions in the brain, namely, *P*lanning to prefrontal cortex, *A*ttention to prefrontal cortex and reticular system (arousal), *S*uccessive to prefrontal cortex and temporal cortex, and simultaneous to posterior brain, namely, parietal and occipital cortices.

To date, emotional phenomenon has not scientifically defined either. Above all, a clear distinction, if any, between emotion and cognition has not been definitely established. In the past, the emotion has been considered just sensitivity independent of any cognitive phenomenon [James, 1890; Schachter, & Singer, 1962]. Later on, the physiological reaction associated to painful-emotional processing was proposed to be unspecific, independent of the concrete painful experience [Lyons, 1980]. More recently, the so-called "appraisal" of the processed painful sensitivity has been claimed to be the primary-determinant reason for any emotional behavior, which points to sensitivity rather than cognition as causal explanation; however, "appraisal" involves belief processing and beliefs are cognitive knowledge supposed to be cognitively processed. Additionally, this last notion is claimed to be applicable to emotional "order" and emotional "disorder" [Power & Dalgleish, 1997] without distinction.

Putting aside the conceptual dualism emotion-cognition, other important notions have to be noted. First, unconscious feeling processing is a generally assumed reality and, for instance, anger can be considered a reactive painful behavior unconsciously triggered [Lyons, 1980]. Second, reactive painful behaviors can be also considered a protective-defensive mechanism beyond any psychodynamic conceptualization [Lazarus, 1966; Horowitz, 1990]. Third, body language and, in particular, the facial expression is universally accepted to automatically-unconsciously express the feeling state of any person [Darwin, 1965; Ekman, 1973; Adolphs & Damasio, 2000; Adolphs et al., 2000], although body language can also convey informative cognitive content undoubtedly. And fourth, substantial evidence is that verbal language incoherent with both body language and physiological reaction proves to be characteristic of the painful emotional-feeling behavioral response [Lang, 1984].

We state that any theoretical framework to explain both cognition and emotion needs to be coherent with the neurological processing evidence we count on at present. Regarding emotion, the first evidence is that physical pain processing and painful emotional processing share, at least in part, anatomical areas and physiological functions. So, it is well known the shared ACTH – endorphin physiological reaction to both physical and emotional stress, which allows us to suppose that both the physical and the emotional stress are codified by the neurons as the same entity, in particular, as a danger signal [Selye, 1974; Buchsbaum, 1982]. Recent growing fMRI (functional magnetic resonance) evidence points to this assertion [Cabeza & Nyberg, 2000].

The second evidence is that nowadays we know, although from animal experimentation, the pathways of painful-feeling processing from input to output of information [LeDoux et al., 1984, 1986, 1990; LeDoux, 1995, 1996, 2000]. According to this, painful-fearful sensitivity is unconsciously processed and, more strikingly, controlled by the temporal amygdala, the second gate in the pathway that triggers unconsciously uncontrolled automatic protective-defensive response. The prefrontal cortex knows what is going on later and does not avoid the behavioral reaction, already triggered by the amygdala, to a supposed life-threatening situation.

The third evidence, from human lesion investigation, is that two prefrontal cortex, the emotional and the cognitive, have been dissociated and, strikingly, decision-making and planning faculty seems to basically depend on the emotional prefrontal rather than on the cognitive prefrontal [Damasio, 1994, 1995, 1999] when painful processing occurs, which allows us to reasonably deduce that the emotional sensitivity processing is a priority, even though the higher cognitive function is on. And a fourth subsequent evidence is that planning and feeling are interactive processing [Goldberg, 2001]. All these points will be discussed later on.

And to end this section, we will comment on the following important point. Defining how much of a behavioral pattern is due to innate-genetic factor versus adquired-enviromental factor is a crucial point to be discussed if only briefly. The study by Bouchard in the Minnesota Center for Twin and Adoption Research showed that the genetic factor (genotype) gets to account for 40 to 60 % of the behavioral pattern (phenotype). Recently, it has been reported that 35% of monozygotic twin brothers sharing the same genotype, pertaining to a sample of more than 100 pairs, showed different phenotype [Proceeding of the National Academy of Sciences, 2005]. If so, given that the adquired component seems to be more significant than the congenital one, then the assertion that what is learnt can be unlearnt becomes a key point for the treatment of dysfunctional situations.

In sum, we must keep in mind that the behavior we study must be considered the output of information processing. Therefore, the information enters via the senses, is centrally processed at neurological centers, and leaves via the motor system with verbal or non-verbal expression. In turn, the central neurological centers constitute a serial network from the sensorial input to the motor output with the higher processor in between [Mesulam, 1987,1998, 2000] We can observe input and output, but so far we can just deduce the central processing, although the neuroimage most modern techniques are allowing us to begin observing the central processing. Fortunately, we are going beyond the behaviorism [Hebb,1949, 1968].

Chapter 3

INFORMATION PROCESSING

As we are saying, knowing information processing at the neurological level is essential to understand how behavior happens. Our framework is based on the PASS information processing concept. The *P*lanning, *A*ttention, *S*imultaneous and *S*uccessive (PASS) cognitive processing model is described as a modern theory to explain learning and intelligent behavior. It is about information processing that is a dynamic process and not a static ability. It is based on Luria's analyses of functional brain structures. The four processes work in the context of an individual's knowledge base.

As we had advanced, each processing is supported by a neurological network being associated with a particular part of the brain; Planning with prefrontal lobe, Attention with brainstem and prefrontal lobe, Successive with temporal lobe and frontal lobe and Simultaneous with posterior brain, that is, occipital and parietal lobe. Planning mental activity must be emphasized. Planning process will be required when the individual makes some decision about how to solve a problem, carry out an activity such as how to write an essay about the last summer vacation, or what to say to a friend who has lost his father.

Mainly, Planning allows us to foresee the consequences following any act we do, which involves decision-making. Planning is also needed both to focus our attention and to use simultaneous and successive processes when required. Planning has been described as a hierarchical neuronal network [Dehaene et al. 1997; Van den Heuvel, 2005], and has to do with executive function [Stuss & Benson, 1986; Shallice, 1988; Welsh & Penninton, 1988; Fuster, 1989]. Simultaneous processing has to do with the mental activity to process relations, associations and spatial processing. Successive processing allows us to mentally operate with a serial relationship, no other relationship being processed.

We have already exemplified the integral mental activity of learning with PASS processing, by resorting to the mental activity to remember 633435. Remember you may do it recalling the series with no other association but just only the lineal association, one digit with the following. If so, you are operating with successive processing. Instead, you can do it recalling as 63 34 35 in which case you are using successive processing for recording three units, that is, 63 / 34 / 35 but each unit has been mentally elaborated with simultaneous processing. Furthermore, you can think as previously expressed but also you think 63 / 34 / 35 is as if 34, 35 and 36 in consecutive order but turning 36 into 63 and translating the last unit to the first unit in the series. In such a case planning allows you to operate this mental strategy. Attention processing is always present. We would recommend that this example be kept in mind.

Every processing is a mental activity independent of input and output of information, although visual input tends to be processed simultaneously and auditive input successively. Input and output, either verbal or manipulative, may be both successive and simultaneous, but both input and output may be successive and, instead, central processing simultaneous. This concept of mental cognitive operation allows us to intervene, for instance, on a dyslexic problem without using reading as a training material, something we are recalling through our discussion. In fact, reading is a behavioral output and we know the PASS processes are utilized by our brain whatever behavior is put in action beyond any other consideration [Delacato, 1966].

Terms as auditive discrimination, phonologic processing, receptive language, expressive language, visual perception, auditive sequential memory, verbal memory, visual memory, short-term memory, long-term memory can all be accounted for in the light of PASS cognitive processing. Each of these terms corresponds to the description of something we externally observe any human being is able to do. Under every descriptive term, we assume a mental activity is operating as responsible for the result we call, for instance, phonologic processing but frequently we don't know exactly which activity is underway [Narbona & Chevrie-Muller, 1996].

Since Luria's lesion studies [Luria, 1980], further lesion studies [Damasio, 1994,1995, 1999; Camile et al. 2004, Perez-Alvarez et al. 2006c] have replicated the Luria's results, and lately modern functional neuroimage studies [Cabeza & Nyberg, 2000] are confirming those results. For instance, both a complex mental arithmetic task and a task consisting of strategic searching for a missing card within a pack of cards activate the dorsolateral prefrontal cortex. Two apparent different tasks are resolved by the same neuronal area. We assume an area always sets up the same functional programs. As concordant evidence, factorial analysis demonstrates planning is involved in both tasks. Studies like these prove that dorsolateral prefrontal is implied in planning processing. On the contrary, two tasks like which number is between 3 and 5 and which day is between Monday and Wednesday behave differently. These two apparent conceptually similar tasks do not activate the same neurological areas. The first task activates left parietal, whereas the second one does the non-parietal area. Of course, the factorial analysis demonstrates the involvement of different PASS processes.

Moreover, functional neuroimage studies [Cebeza & Nyberg, 2000] have contributed to distinguishing the peripheral sensorial network from the central high-order network, according to the PASS principle. For instance, to recite multiplication tables by heart activates parietal and temporal. Factorial analysis demonstrates the involvement of simultaneous. The associative parietal cortex is linked to simultaneous processing and temporal lobe to successive, but also to primary sensorial neurons processing auditive sensation or perception. In this sense, functional neuroimage studies of language have been clearly illustrative, demonstrating how both receptive-perceptive areas (e.g., Wernicke) and expressive-motor areas (e.g.Broka) can be differentiated from central high-order areas. Broca area operates even in the case of silent reading, which means that Broca's neurons are successively placed in the processing network before the somatic neurons responsible for the motor act of speaking out. Another neurological principle is that the more central, the less the concentration of neurons. In fact, this is in accordance with what was years ago demonstrated by using electrical stimulation of neurons in conscious patients being operated on because of a lesion in brain. With local anesthesia it is possible to test which effect on language follows after the stimulation in different areas of the brain [Penfield & Rasmussen, 1957; Penfield & Perot, 1963; Ojemann, 1976]. Similar functional neuroimage studies with equivalent results have been made by working on music processing.

Multiple studies based not only on functional neuroimage [Raichle, 1998] but also on acoustic analysis of temporal processing of information [Tallal, 1980: Tallal et al.,1993] and on other methods have conclusively shown that central processing is independent of input and output of information, just as the essential principle of the PASS theory affirms.

The DN:CAS battery was created to assess intelligence in the sense of PASS cognitive processing. As we have remarked, its construction from neurological theoretical conception has been different from that of historical tests made to assess cognitive function. Nonverbal tests as the Wechles, Binet 4, K-ABC, and McCarthy can be analyzed according to the PASS concept. In addition to nonverbal tests, current IQ tests also have a large number of measures that involve verbal content. These can be also analyzed according to the PASS concept. Processing speed is taken into account with the introduction of the WISC-III so, as planning tests are timed, some could argue these measures are better described as processing speed, but processing speed is not PASS processing. The relationship between the PASS model and the K-ABC warrants particular considerations due to the association the authors of the K-ABC have made with PASS cognitive processing. The K-ABC measures partially both simultaneous and successive processes but not attention and planning. These comments lead us to the next issue of our discussion.

TESTING

A relevant practical point has to do with testing. Nowadays, we know that the IQ in the population has been gaining 0.3 point per year since the standardization of Stanford Binet (1932) and WISC (1948) [Flynn, 1984]. Ideally, any test must fulfil validity and reliability. Validity means accuracy in the sense the test measures what it is supposed to measure. Reliability means consistency, that is, the same measurement every time is given to the same person. The higher the error of validity or/and reliability, the lower the validity or/and the reliability of the test will be. In turn, validity and reliability of any test are linked to sensibility and specificity. The higher the sensibility, the lower the number of false positive results. The higher the specificity, the lower the number of false negative results. We are used to seeing that a particular test is assumed to measure several considered different cognitive functions. So, for instance, Stroop and Trail Making tests are considered valid to assess both attention and executive function.

We must insist that what a particular test measures depends on the theoretical framework it is based on. Neurological evidence and mathematical validation are the two mainstays of the PASS conception. When the majority of cognitive tests have been created working on the principle of we know human beings are able of doing something we can assess and later standardize, the PASS conception and the DN:CAS battery was elaborated starting from the analysis of how the brain works on the basis of lesion analysis [Luria, 1980]. In essence, this analysis concluded that what our external observation tells us is different or equal is not always different or equal in the eyes of the neuron. This way, tasks were made and compared with previously existing tasks to discriminate by using factor analysis to see what was equal and what was different. Afterwards, the tasks were standardized.

So, the DN:CAS has been compared with other tests. As a result, we can summarize that: (a) Non-verbal tests of K-ABC, Wechsler, Binet 4 and McCarthy assess simultaneous and sometimes other PASS processing, but also something non-PASS; (b) Verbal tests of K-ABC, Wechsler, Binet 4 and McCarthy measure more than one PASS processing and sometimes something non-PASS; (c) Regarding memory tasks, Forward Span assesses successive, but Backward Span measures successive and planning; (d) Concerning executive function, Wisconsin Cards assess planning, but also something non-PASS; (e) As to attention, Stroop assesses PASS attention. (f) The successive and simultaneous K-ABC match with PASS successive and simultaneous.

In turn, the validity and reliability of any test depends on the scientific method it is likewise based on. Any specific test or subtest must be scientifically verified for us to accurately know what it is measuring. If not, mistake and bias is highly probable. For instance, "A is higher than B, B is higher than C. Which one is higher? Which one lower? " is resolved by using PASS simultaneous processing. Instead, "A is higher than B, C is higher than A, B is higher than C. True or false?" is resolved by using PASS planning [Das et al.,1994, 1996]. Also, to get to reach a toy that is far away behind an obstacle by removing the obstacle and pulling the fabric where the object is placed is a behavior a 9-month-old infant can do. We can see this behavior involves some kind of strategy, but it has been scientifically (factorial analysis) verified that this action does not demand PASS planning, a processing that is not operative before 5 years old.

Planning is efficiency. Efficiency is accuracy plus speed, but not solely speed. Therefore the tests, like verbal fluency or those based on reaction time, using only speed of processing to assess executive function do not measure PASS planning function. They assess another cognitive function we do not know exactly.

Attention processing deserves a particular comment. PASS attention processing may be considered equivalent to what we know as selective attention. Immediately, we must say that another kind of defined attention functions, like sustained attention, dual or divided attention, supervising anterior attention, perceptive posterior attention, and attention of continuous performance task can not be defined in terms of PASS processing. In PASS terms, selective attention is a controlling voluntary function sinilar to planning function, both of them linked to prefrontal cortex capability. The rest of the attentions we have just mentioned do not load in any factor corresponding to PASS processing or jointly loads in some PASS and non-PASS factor, when factor analysis is made. For instance, a non-automatic visual search task involves PASS planning and automatic visual search does otherwise not linked to PASS processing. This is in accordance with what fMRI or PET studies (functional neuroimage studies) tells us: parietal, linked in PASS terms to simultaneous, is involved in automatic visual searching.

We will go on with a brief discussion of memory. The PASS processes are not memories, but memory works using the PASS processes. The matter is that verbal memory, auditive memory, and visual memory are different kinds of memories defined by the input of information, that is, we apply a distinctive term, depending on which entrance is operating. In turn, short-term memory, long-term memory, episodic memory, biographic memory are defining terms on the basis of some circumstance involved in the mental task. The situation is not different from those cases of number processing, mental arithmetic processing, language processing, vocabulary processing, semantic processing, syntactic processing, phonologic processing, pragmatic processing, discourse processing, music processing, and so on. From the PASS view, what is relevant is that the PASS processing is operating whenever any of the previously mentioned cognitive functions is working.

Even very recent neuropsychological batteries [Matute et al. 2005] continue to be constructed according to traditional method producing tasks of lecture, receptive and expressive language, attention, construction, space, memory, visual and auditive perception, conceptualization, executive function, and metacognition. On administering these batteries, we tend to find some inconsistencies because of the inconsistency of the framework.

We must insist that information processing has to do with memory, but it is not memory. It is well known we recall by association of ideas (PASS simultaneous), but rote memorization (PASS successive) is also needed at least at to a minimum. All mnemonic devices are based on this. Some principles or rules have been described: similarity - difference or contrast or space-time association. For instance, to memorize the series "water, salt, sugar, oil, butter, milk", we can memorize it by resorting to the similarity - difference principle as "water-oil, salt-sugar, milk-butter". Or for memorizing "home, Peter, beach, pier, old, south", we can do it by resorting to "Peter's home is near beach where the old pier in the south". Any association can be established as the case of acronyms (for instance, PASS) or chunking (transforming 633435 into 63 34 35). Having stated these considerations about testing, we will deal with language processing and logic application as an key aspect of cognitive processing.

LANGUAGE PROCESSING AND LOGIC

One comment that we should make now is about language processing. Language is PASS processed, but furthermore it deserves an additional comment. Language is the linguistic form of human thought and it must be considered an artificial construction based on conventional signs with operational meaning (Balmes, 1968). In essence, however, the linguistic form of human thought can be psycholinguistically formulated in terms of A is / is not B or A has / has not B or A does / does not B in the most simple construction. Indeed, in this sense grammar is governed by innate rules [Chomsky 1986]. Ordinarily, however, the construction is in formal grammar formulated in a more complex way in terms of A is / is not B or A has / has not B or A does / does not B + [determiner]. The [determiner] is any object or complement in way of words, phrase or clause. It has to do with purpose, cause, time, place, and so on. In fact, the *determiner* becomes a *condition* in terms of logical deduction.

For instance, "It is very important this in order to (purpose clause) get that." "You may have this because (causal clause) you deserve it." "When (temporal clause) you get it, I'll reward you." "I found it where (place clause) you live." "If (conditional clause) you come, I will go." All these examples show how a main statement is followed or preceded by a circumstantial clause, but essentially the linguistic construction is mentally processed as the statement happens on condition that the circumstantial clause happens.

Having said that, we must add something about logic. Language conveys thoughts and thoughts explicitly but also implicitly work according to rules of thinking that are the rules of deductive reasoning. In fact, the so-called inductive reasoning may be considered a form of deductive reasoning with suppressed premises [Shand, 2000]. A rational process is one that obeys the laws of logic. For instance: "All are X, this is X, therefore this is what all are." An irrational process is one that breaks the laws of logic. For instance. "All are X, this is what all, therefore this is Y". A non-rational process is one that can not be said either to obey or to break the laws of logic. For instance: "This is not what I want". Likewise, inductive reasoning may be formulated as: "This is X + another this is X + another this is X = All are X; this one is X, therefore this one is like All".

Good reasoning implies that the premises must be true and the argument valid so that the conclusion follows from the premises. Therefore, the good logical reasoning consists of using only valid arguments and true premises; for only in this way does an argument give a reason to the conclusion being true. Then, validity is a matter of form and so the good reasoning is a matter of form. To discover the truth of the premises is a key question. The beliefs are part of the premises and the beliefs are more frequently implicit than explicit. And of course the beliefs are important determinants of our actions. We believe certain things and then we act on those beliefs. [Balmes, 1964; Shand, 2000].

Taking this into account, it makes sense that seductive psychological factors prevent us from reasoning, that psychological rhetorical tricks, that psychological blindness induced by factors outside where the reasoning process operates, that understanding reason is not enough because psychological factors undermine our ability to argue well, that knowing is frequently not sufficient, that what convinces people has often little or nothing to do with the quality of the arguments with which they are presented, that an outstanding logician may hold strange and implausible reasoning based on particular beliefs. Definitely, we can assert that emotion reactions are perfectly reasonable and, if so, we are purely logical creatures. We may consider a misconception that living rationally involves negating and suppressing our emotions all the time.

It is said that emotions are considered one of the major causes of our failing to think rationally and that we may need to set emotion aside and consider the arguments, but the aracnophobe may rationally know that the spider is not dangerous, but may nevertheless be unable to apply reason to his fearful beliefs about spiders. From the point of view of successful intervention, we must bring up how much of the emotional reaction is instinctive, how much acquired.

Non-good logical reasoning appears whenever the behavior being expressed is not the consequence of logical reasoning supported by cognitive neocortex, but of the unconscious bad feeling supported by subneocortical amygdala network processing a danger signal due to past painful experiences. This is in accordance with the non-physical painful-fear processing in animal experimentation [LeDoux et al., 1984, 1986, 1990; LeDoux, 1995,1996, 2000]. Recently, stathmin, a gene enriched in the amygdala, that controls both learned and innate fear has been reported [Shumyatsky et al. 2005].

As we will discuss later on, the key concept is that, whenever and whatever behavior is put in action, both cognitive (ideas) and feeling (sensitivity) processing happen at a neurological level. The behavior in action is essentially the consequence of feeling processing rather than of cognitive processing, which is what our fMRI study [Perez-Alvarez et al. 2006b] tells us. It is also what lesion studies tell us [Damasio, 1994,1995, 1999; Camile et al. 2004, Perez-Alvarez et al. 2006c].

For instance, a patient with an emotional prefrontal lesion behaves unsociably because his/her emotional medial-ventral-inferior prefrontal is not processing-codifying painful feeling associated with behaving unsociably, but not because his/her cognitive dorsolateral prefrontal along with his/her temporal, parietal and occipital external cognitive cortices are unable of understanding which consequence follows which behavior. In other words, if I behave sociably, I really do it because I will feel badly otherwise, but not for exactly any reason of understanding, learning, or reasoning. In other words, the behavior is coherent with feeling, but not with good logical reasoning, if enough painful-feeling takes place.

Cerebral cortex makes a conscious argument to externally express the unconscious painful feeling processing. Really, we postulate that the cerebral cortex, it once has received the non-informative data signal of danger coming from the amygdala, puts in action a behavior, resorting to the previously memorized knowledge coming from the personal historical past of the patient for reasons we can not explain yet. Experience tells us this is true not only for somatization, but also for any masked reactive painful behavior which we will talk about extensively later on. Usually, the conscious argumentation fails in good logical reasoning.

The failure in good logical reasoning can be verified in (a) contradiction between verbal language and body language, (b) contradiction in arguments of verbal language, if only in causal reasons argued, (c) disproportional cause-effect relationship susceptible to be seen in overacting verbal or/and body behavior (exaggerating-overreacting-disproportional behavior for the causal-effect reason either explicitly or implicitly argued), and (d) cognitive PASS planning dysfunction. More extensively, we will return to this subject in the Guideline chapter. Next, linking with language and logic, we must now proceed to dealing with another language, the body language.

BODY LANGUAGE

Body language, including para-verbal language, is an older communication system than verbal language. From the cognitive point of view, verbal language comes out in order for human beings to communicate complex concepts-ideas. More simple cognitive content can be efficiently communicated by means of body language. Body language is present in the history of life since early times and, likewise, the defensive-protective system based on the pain processing has been operative for obvious reasons. From the beginning living beings resorted to body language, to communicate something cognitively and sensitively susceptible to be processed, as an instrument to respond efficiently in case of danger processing (Ekman, 1973; Adolphs & Damasio, 2000; Adolphs et al., 2000), whether physical or non-physical. Body language is unconsciously triggered in case of danger processing, which accounts for the incoherence between body language and verbal language (actions do not match words) whenever it occurs (Lang, 1984). Bodies talk, just as words do.

Body – gesture language was the first system of communication in the history of life. At the beginning, the living cell needed to externally express the reaction to "feeling" and the available tool was body language. As verbal language developed, the para-verbal language (a way of body language) formed part of it. Later on, year after year and century after century, the body language continued to convey feeling. Verbal language is the most modern system of communication created to convey ideas and concepts and it is generated by the cognitive cortical neurons.

At present, the most recent fMRI neurological evidence confirms that verbal language and body language are processed in different neurological regions (Adolph et al. 2000). Today, it is universally assumed that uncontrolled body language unconsciously expresses feeling and, in particular, bad feeling (Darwin, 1965; Ekman, 1973; Adolphs & Damasio, 2000; Adolphs et al.2000). On the contrary, verbal language is not created to transmit feeling that is a sensitivity. As experience demonstrates, the sensitivity is better communicated by body language as is the case of body contact for expressing feeling.

Body language informs us about both cognitive and feeling processing. For instance, a strategy, we can observe, for 2+4 can be a verbal or subvocal count strategy: three, three… four, four…five, five…six…. Then, 6. Or also a child is spelling a word; he/she sounds the constituent letters, then says "Now that's …," takes a deep breath, and reads the word aloud. This strategy gives him/her an extra two or three seconds to think of an answer. Something similar to the "thinking out loud" strategy, that is, to rehearse or repeat information to facilitate remembering (successive / working memory). We know also that the internalization process may be accompanied by the ah! exclamation [Bhüler, 1907]. Suddenly the child has an insight. For instance, a child is questioned:"What comes after nine?" Silence follows. I say: "1,2,3,4,5,6,7,8,9 …" And he/she says: ah! (insight). And adds: "10". Or may be: "Oh, so that's it!"

Or eye language may be very informative. For instance, eyes up and to the left or to the right indicates simultaneous processing, eyes level and to the left or to the right successive processing, eyes down and to the left or to the right body sensations. And other body expressions are informative: wrinkled forehead and/or contracted jaw and/or shoulders thrown back and/or breathing shallow and in the chest and/or a fixed grin indicate tension - concentration. On the contrary, shoulders relaxed and drooped breathing deeply in abdominal area as breathing from diaphragm indicates tranquility, relaxation.

Therefore, many body expressions tell us about cognition and emotion: unusual posture, specific hand movements, head turns, leaning to one side, rocking back and forth or side to side, rigid body, facial expression (mouth and eyebrows), startled look, big grin on the face, eye contact, yawning, particular words or phrases, voice quality and pitch, tone, volume, inflection, speed, tempo (rhythmic, choppy), and so on. We are not interested so much in what someone is saying as in how it is being said. At this point, it is high time we stress the importance of beliefs and their learning and memorization.

LEARNING, KNOWLEDGE BASE AND BELIEFS

We can explain how learning happens by understanding how information processing is carried out. The simplest learning, consisting of memorizing many apparently isolated facts, is rote memorization, which plays an important role in the initial stages of learning. For instance, preschoolers often first learn to use numbers mechanically, or by trial-and-error problem solving, and then gradually discover or construct deeper and deeper understanding. In PASS terms, rote memorization is mainly linked to successive processing.

Learning is a process of memorization, but meaningful learning is a different process from learning by rote memorization. Children may accurately imitate computational routines without understanding. Understanding is learning by insight. Insight requires thought. For instance, meaning of the plus sign (+) or minus sign (-) or times sign (x) or equals sign (=) happens by connecting the symbols to their concept. From the beginning, associations - relationships take place. In PASS terms, association is simultaneous. This way, thinking skill matures to reach deductive reasoning or the use of rules or principles to logically prove points. The discovery of relationships by examining cases characterizes inductive insight. In PASS terms, this operation implies planning.

Forming associations involves making connections with existing knowledge. Initially, the existing knowledge has to do with informal knowledge linked to personal experience. Informal knowledge is basically a concrete-tangible knowledge. Meaningful learning is necessarily dependent on what an individual already knows, and it takes place by relating the formal knowledge (symbolism, definition, and so on) to real knowledge (objects, things). Anyone is prone to forget information that is not personally meaningful. Thus, knowledge base becomes a reality. Therefore the role of memorized knowledge base is substantial for learning.

With development [Piaget,1964; Erickson 1991; Kohlberg, 1992], children learn more relationships and their knowledge forms a more complete logical system (knowledge becomes more interconnected) to reason deductively, applying general abstracted principles or rules to solve specific problems. Children evolve from the simpler form of learning by rote memorization to more complex forms of learning and thinking (planning). Gradually, they are able to manage more cognitively complicated tasks. They reach a more advanced stage in thinking ability. For instance, counting backward is more difficult than counting forward for young children. Or at about 3 years children discover that higher count term is associated with larger magnitude. They realize that 2 not only follows 1 but also represents a larger quantity than does 1. It is well known that language, weather verbal or written, is understood by the listener or reader according to the meaning shared by the transmitter and receptor of the language [Just & Carpenter, 1987; Kintsch, 1988; Caplan, 1992]. Reality is a tough concept. Truth is even worse. Both are incredibly elusive and totally dependent on the frame of reference (knowledge base). Beliefs become an important part of the knowledge base.

In essence, relationship learning has to do with discriminating "same as" (equivalence) from "different from" (inequivalence). That's why discrimination is more difficult in cases of high similarity. The more defining characteristics that are shared, the more likely that a child or any person will be confused. For instance, for a child learning reading, letters like "f" and "t" or "n" and "h", and "p" and "b" and "d". Also, numbers like 6 and 9. This discrimination is based on cognitive network higher complex than perceptual - motor network, which is involved in fine -visual - motor integration processing responsible for the proper coordination of eyes and hand movements [Mesulan, 1998].

Before proceeding with other notions, we must clarify how we understand the information neurological processing of beliefs (Das, 1999; Das et al., 1994, 1996, 2000; Perez-Alvarez & Timoneda, 2004). Remember that the PASS processes operate at a central level between input and output, as well as the beliefs likewise work at a central level between input and output. The central-neurological processing happens more frequently unconsciously than consciously between the either consciously or unconsciously processed sensorial input (stimulus) and the either consciously or unconsciously processed output (response).

For instance, a child is presented with single separated letters, concretely, "u, b, s," (consciously processed input). He/she is asked to pronounce the successive combination "b, u, s," and he/she answers (output) correctly (consciously processed output). Then, he/she is asked to pronounce the presented sequence "q, u, s," and the answer (output) is again /bus/. Incorrect answer, but incorrect reasoning? If we ask him/her: "How did you do it?" He/she will answer: "I did it this way" (conscious processed output).

His/her explanation will be elaborated by his/her thinking brain taking via sensorial gates the information coming from outside in real time. In fact, is a posteriori response to the answer being formulated? It is about a posteriori conscious thinking response with respect to the first previous unconscious mechanisms responsible for the resolution of the task. Probably, the verbal explanation being reported (consciously processed) will not correspond to the real reason for the response (unconsciously processed). Really, his/her unconsciously processed knowledge, that is, belief, not susceptible to be consciously and verbally reported, is the symbol "b" sounds /b / whether right side up or not. Then, correct reasoning happened.

So the determinant reason for the behavior was the central unconscious belief. Just only changing this belief the behavior will change subsequently. We must remark that the mental processing we are explaining is in accordance with what the neurological evidence tell us about the painful feeling processing concerning the temporal amygdala and the emotional prefrontal, concretely, the medial-ventral-inferior prefrontal [Damasio, 1994, 1995, 1999; Greene et al., 2001; Singer et al., 2004; Camille et al., 2004; Bechara, 2004].

If the same error in identification persists, we may shake our head in disbelief, unable to understand how the error could persist despite repeated correction. However, there must be a logical reason for him/her reading incorrectly. They do not make mistakes without good reason.

We produce three cards for three letters, namely, "a, b, and c", each one with a different letter and we place them in a row as "cab". Our pupil sounds /kaeb/. Right. Then we place them in a row as "cap". Our pupil sounds /kaeb/ again. Apparently, nonsensical answers. He/she is sounding the figure such that "b" is equal to "p" independently of the position in space. Or we place them as "bac" and he/she strikingly sounds /kaeb/. If so, he/she is merely sounding the position occupied by the card, the left position is called /k/, the middle position /ae/, and the one on the right /b/, regardless another consideration. In fact, mommy is mommy whether you look at her from the front or back, whether your view is right side up or upside down.

Or a child is presented with the subtraction 19 - 8 and 18 - 9 and the answer produced in both cases is 11. He/she obtained the difference between single digit terms but always subtracted the smaller from the larger. This answer is coherent with the belief "always subtract the smaller from the larger". "Peter looks at Jim" and "Jim looks at Peter" contain the same words, but the relationships among the words are different. A sentence must be read as a whole to learn its meaning. Likewise, a multidigit numeral is a number sentence that encodes relationships among individual digits to signify a number. It must be read as a whole to learn its meaning. For instance, 58 is "filthy-eight" but not "five eight". The principle or belief is "order and place determine meaning". In other words, it is needed to decode the information specified by position (order and place).

Evaluation that exclusively examines the resulting product is not accurate, and even may overestimate a child's competence in case of "false success" in academic learning. For instance, with a choice of only two answers to a question, you have a 50-50 chance of getting any particular question right just by guessing. On average, guessing should permit a pupil to get about 5 of the 10 correct. In fact, a correct response does not guarantee a deep appreciation of the rule, principle or belief depending on what we are dealing with. For instance, use of the cardinality rule (stating the last number counted in response to how-many question) does not guarantee a deep appreciation of cardinality.

A focus on performance overlooks invaluable information needed to diagnose incomplete or inaccurate understanding or reasoning and to design an effective remedial plan whether academic maths or behavioral performance is about.. Errors provide important clues about underlying processes and the meaning of errors can disclose we are in the presence of a "false failure." Practically, we are always facing rule-governed learning. They are logical, although incorrect. Next, we will focus our discussion on how the intervention must be understood.

FOUNDATION OF DIAGNOSIS AND TREATMENT

The construction of beliefs is learning. The change of beliefs is also learning. Belief can be substituted for knowledge and knowledge for informative data content, whether abstract or concrete, whether linguistic language or body language. Definitely, it is about learning phenomenon independently of the context and learning is information processing.

You may teach reading, making the learner see the letters a, b, and c, and later sounding /ei/, /bee/, /see/ This so-called phonic method involves a low quantity of associations (simultaneous processing) and instead a high requirement of rote memory (successive processing), which is more linked to pure repetition to improve with doing as an automatically produced mechanical behavior or mechanical thinking. This learning based on facilitating rote memory by repetition is not an efficient one. The more efficient learning is founded on minimizing successive processing (working memory / short term memory) and maximizing simultaneous processing (associations / long term memory) by tutored training planning (strategies / problem solving / decision-making). For instance, a regrouping strategy like 46+38 = [40+30] + [6+8] = 85 is a useful one to minimize the load on working memory. Making chunks of information works similarly. And so many examples.

Indeed, tutored training is superior to non-tutored training, which is more linked to intuitive learning. Nearly all children 3-year-olds entering school are able to distinguish between and label as "more" the larger of two obviously different sets. The child uses "more" in a intuitive manner basing the judgement on appearance. Although appearance often accurately reflects amount, perceptual cues are not always accurate indicators of either number or knowledge.

The intuitive learning leading to intuitive knowledge fits into the existing pattern of thought. Young children, for instance, presented with a container with 5 items and another with 9 to which we add 4 and 2 more items respectively, think 5 + 4 is "more than" 9 + 2 because they saw "more" added to the first container. Clearly, intuitive arithmetic is imprecise, but the performance is coherent with the belief. Also, by observing that adding objects to a set "makes more", a child intuitively concludes that when a coin is added to a cup with five coins, that cup then contains more than a cup of eight to which nothing has been added. Or a child concludes that his longer row of 7 has more than his shorter row of 8 is using perceptual criterion of length to conclude that the longer row has more quantity. He/she must realize that the number of items in a set does not change because the appearance of the set has changed. The work of making the child internalize and transfer the new knowledge that substitutes the old knowledge (change of belief) is the aim of an efficient intervention.

This efficient intervention requires much more than just practice. Practice in itself does not guarantee learning. We must concisely discuss the role of repetition on learning according to neurological evidence. We know that signal transmission through synapsis is facilitated by the repetition of activity of the synapsis [Guyton, 1971.pp. 580; Guyton & Hall, 1996]. Since we know the long-term potentiation phenomenon [Hebb, 1949, 1968], we also know that the effect of a stimulus becomes more potent when previous stimuli have been applied.

Therefore repetition works by itself, but obviously temporal summation-rote memorization is a mental activity less efficient than global PASS mental processing. The spatial summation phenomenon must be considered a neuronal expression of simultaneous processing. And conditioning is simultaneous processing and consequently learning may be considered as a conditioning phenomenon [Bolles, 1975a, 1975b].

Practice is important to make thinking skills automatic once learning takes place. Empirical evidence indicates that the amount of practice (pointless drills, interviews, conversations) is not predictive of mastery. On the contrary, mastery is more directly linked to the development of meaningful knowledge than to practice frequency, although you'll learn by doing, by performing. It may take time to see, assimilate new information to what is known, and build up a network of relationships. Whereas some relationships are relatively easy to see and are quickly internalized (comprehension), others are not easily abstracted and require time to master. In achieving this aim, understanding painful feeling processing may be capital. Children go at their own pace. Moreover, it is very frustrating for children to continue practicing when they can see that they are doing it incorrectly but do not know how to correct it.

Next, we will present a series of examples of how planning training [Das et al, 1996; Das et al. 2000] operates in order to get to construct or change a strategy. We must insist that what is said of strategy is applicable to belief.

A boy, 4 or 5 years old, counts 10 pebbles in a row. Then, he counts them again in the opposite direction. Again he finds 10. Now, he arranges the pebbles in a circle, counts them and once more finds 10. Finally, the boy counts the circle of pebbles in the opposite direction only to find the arrangement of elements and the order in which they are counted are irrelevant in determining the result [Piaget, 1964].

For the problem 2+4, the following concrete procedure can be used. One finger extended is 3, two fingers extended are 4, three fingers extended are 5, and four fingers extended are 6. Then, 2+4 = 6. This keeping-track process requires little attention (working memory) and thus can be executed quite efficiently.

When the minuend and subtrahend are relatively close, as in 8-6, counting-up minimizes the working memory demand, that is, two steps (seven, eighth) as opposed with counting down, which requires six steps (seven, six, five, four, three, two).

A child experiences that, for instance, 5-4 = 1; 8-7 = 1; 23-22 = 1. The child may realize that the answer is always one. Then the rule: "the subtraction of two number neighbors produces a difference of one" can be internalized and transferred. The children can abstract a general rule or principle that enables them to respond efficiently even to previously unencountered problem (far transfer). Inductive learning works from the concrete and specific to the abstract and general. The abstract principle is to find something common to all the items. Abstraction is a question of degree such that the higher degree of abstraction is required for the higher cognitive concept.

A child may learn a procedure mechanically (rote memory / rotely memorized) but not really understand why the procedure works. This is non meaningful learning, a senseless procedure where the lack of relationships or associations does not make far transfer possible and achievable. The new knowledge is not internalized to be used (transferred) in a new task. The mechanical use of rotely learned procedures means that the rotely learned rules cannot transfer. Children fail to see any connection with a known procedure.

Obviously, a concrete strategy becomes inefficient, even impossible, according to what is required. We can use concrete procedures like blocks, fingers or marks for 5-2. That is, for problems with addends of 5 or less, for instance, a finger-pattern procedure can be useful. So, for 3+5, a child puts up finger patterns of 3 and 5 on separate hands and then counts all 8 fingers. However, this strategy cannot be used with problems, such as 3+9 and 4+10. If so, another efficient mental computing procedure, the most economical mental procedure to minimize cognitive effort, is needed. A child may have no difficulty with 4x2 by doing four counted two times, but he may be overwhelmed by the problem 2x4 by doing two counted four times. He needs to see that 4x2 is equivalent to 2x4, that is, that multiplication is commutative (Commutativity rule: 6+3 = 3+6). When ready, children will abandon concrete procedures in favor of mental procedures.

Regarding comprehension, the child should be weaned from activities that rely on concrete objects (using concrete objects to compute the sum, for instance), visible clues (by pushing counted objects away into a clearly separate pile), and so on, and required to solve the problems mentally, gradually going from concrete to abstract representation, and running the bridge between concrete but limited direct perception and abstract but general ideas. In fact, this principle is applicable to any learning independently of the context (academic learning, behavioral dysfunction), so both PASS planning training intervention and behavioral dysfunction intervention must take into account it. We will see how the metaphor as an excellent tool of empathic communication runs the bridge between concrete and abstract ideas.

Procedural rules that are not understood are sometimes only partially remembered or remembered incorrectly because the understanding rationale is lacking. If they lack conceptual knowledge, they may deal with a new task in terms of their existing procedural knowledge. Thus they may use inappropriate, partially correct, or invented procedures on a regular basis for an extended period of time so that the systematic errors remain consistent or stable. Whether we are dealing with academic learning or behavioral dysfunction, this assertion is true.

Even children with learning difficulties can see ways of using their existing knowledge to shortcut cognitive effort, inventing more efficient workable strategies (planning), more powerful mental strategies. The same is true for very young or disadvantaged or mentally handicapped children [Perez-Alvarez et al. 1999]. Concerning math learning as a practical example, we know that multiplication is a shortcut (more efficient strategy) for the relatively cumbersome process of repeated addition.

We must consider personal beliefs as rules or principles governing the behavior, which must be considered the answer in terms of information processing. The answer is a product rather than a process. We must diagnose internal thought processes, that is, the how, not the how much (behavioral response). Constructive or healthy beliefs produce pleasant behaviors. For academic learning, for instance, the belief "it is all right not to know everything and to ask questions when help is needed" determines a behavior in response to a question. On the contrary, unconstructive, unreasonable, debilitating beliefs produce painful behaviors. For instance, beliefs like "smart people know everything, only dumb people have to ask questions", "smart people answer quickly", " giving some answer is better than saying, I don't know", "mathematics is something only a genius can comprehend", "mathematics is not supposed to make sense", and so on determine another kind of behavior. Constructive beliefs translate "can" whereas unconstructive beliefs do "can't".

The personal identity is constructed by building the personal beliefs. The personal beliefs operate at central neurological level between input and output of information processing. The personal beliefs are constructed by means of a mental cognitive generally unconscious-implicit process as follows: external information whether verbal, for instance "you are stupid", or non-verbal, for instance "a bad experience at school" or "a bad experience at home", enters via sensorial gates to the central nervous system where a knowledge-belief is constructed. The construction takes place according to the formula "A is/has/have B". For instance, "being intelligent is good, is worthy, is a capability", and immediately an inferential extrapolation unconsciously-implicitly happens that we can formulate as " If being intelligent is worthy, then I am worthy if I am intelligent". This is the cognitive processing leading to belief building that simultaneously is feeling-processed.

With these ideas in mind, we dare to postulate that the highest efficiency of any cognitive training depends more on neuronal network processing feeling than on neuronal network processing cognition. That is, the higher amelioration in cognitive performance after cognitive training may be mainly the consequence of the amelioration in feeling processing.

THE PERSONAL BELIEFS BUILD THE PERSONAL IDENTITY

Diagnosis and intervention in cognition and/or emotion is equivalent to diagnosis and intervention in human being behavior. Cognition, emotion, and behavior are governed by information processing of data and associated feeling processing. The rules of learning are the principles of behavior. Using a previously learned but inappropriate procedure-belief (thought plus feeling processing) produces systematic error in behavior.

Cognition and emotion work together, but painful feeling can provoke planning failure. In fact, the human animal is remarkably good at blinding itself to the obvious if it happens to be unpleasant enough. Planning is a goal, choosing, checking, flexibility, and decision-making as an ongoing problem-solving process. Real unconditioned planning is self-confidence (self-esteem, self-worth) and self-discipline reducing the need to be imposed order by authority, and it is not just following orders. This means the decision (responsibility, choice) is left up to him/her for him/her to gain self-confidence, sef-esteem, and self-worth.

Planning is able to control behavioral drive - impulsivity on condition that painful feeling processing (gut reaction) does not go beyond a limit. When the limit is exceeded, behavior is not the consequence of good logical reasoning consciously-explicitly argued. It appears overexaggerating and inconsistent or nonsensical behavior that are unconsciously produced (masked behavior) [Goleman, 1986]. In these circumstances, the provoking factors or situations are mistakenly identified as the whole responsible for the particular behavior. The accumulated painful feeling linked to the past remains opaque to conscience. A particular behavior (the what) is consciously processed, but its mechanism of production (the how) is unconsciously processed.

The human being behaves defensively with protective behavioral strategies put in action by the neurological centers of fear-danger processing, conveying internal unconscious uncertainty and processing of potential "life-threatening" condition at the neurological level. This state is a suffering state that is experienced unconsciously, subconsciously or consciously depending on the existence of compensating response to the behavior. This is something similar to bodily tension that can be unnoticed or by degrees clearly noticed. When conscious, the protective-defensive behavior becomes painful, anxious, insecure, angry, frustrated, discouraged, afraid or many other applicable terms, all of them stress-related ailments, meaning bad feeling. Under these circumstances, it is not strange that most of our arguments with one another really come down to, who is right? What a useless way to hurt each other's feeling!

At last, feeling processing rules cognitive processing. For instance, a child has difficulties with discriminating "m" from "n". Initially, he/she tries resolving the problem by resorting to his/her strategies. Eventually, he/she has physical discomfort; the bad feelings become more powerful and he/she is more aware of them than of the cognitive strategies. He/she can then no longer see while he/she pays attention to how bad he/she feels. The task at hand becomes less important than feeling badly. He/she really has not a choice by the time he/she feels that way. This way, cognition and emotion work. If you stop breathing, your brain won't care so much about remembering anything except how to stay alive. Try holding your breath for 20 to 30 seconds, and then try to remember the capital of Poland or some equally vital bit of information. Or try and do a math problem in your head while holding your breath. We can similarly apply this discourse by substituting the "m"-"n" discriminating tasks for any other one including any dysfunctional behavior.

More and more neurological evidence points to the fact that the painful-sensitivity feeling processing network count on neurons processing and codifying sensitivity, but not cognitive informative data, even for the prefrontal, the cognitive cerebral lobe par excellence. In fact, this described functional mechanism compares with what we now know about painful-sensitivity feeling processing in animals [LeDoux et al., 1984, 1986, 1990; LeDoux, 1995, 1996, 2000].

Having said that, we must clarify that any person, either consciously or unconsciously experiencing painful feeling, is processing two kinds of bad feeling. One, the past memorized bad feeling linked to what psychologists calls personal identity, and other one the current bad feeling that is generally associated with a concrete current painful event (triggering factor, immediate causal precipitating factor). The memorized painful feeling (sensitivity) is associated with the correspondent cognitive component (informative data) that constitutes the learned and memorized personal beliefs. We are saying through the discussion that the personal beliefs work basically at central subconscious level beyond what we externally can see, hear, etc. between input of information (event or events as precipitant factors) and output of information (behavioral response) [Das, 1999; Das et al. 1994, 1996, 2000; Perez-Alvarez & Timoneda, 2004a, 2004b].

At this point of the discussion, we must tackle the crucial subject of cognition and emotion integration to explain the human behavior as an intelligent product of the mind. We are going to bring up the somewhat critical issue of "I think, then I exist" or, may be, "I feel, then I exist".

Chapter 4

COGNITION AND EMOTION

More and more evidence from not only animal experimentation but also both clinical and functional magnetic resonance image experiences in humans point to the fact that the amygdala is an undifferentiated processor of physical and non-physical feeling-sensitivity, acting whenever an experience implies either good or, preferentially, bad feeling, regardless which term we use for the particular situation. As the pain processing must be considered a defensive-protective system, we will briefly comment on several arguments in favor of the concept of physical pain and non-physical pain as the same neurobiological entity from the point of view that what codifies the neuron is a signal equivalent to danger.

It has always been well known that physical and non-physical pain share some anatomical regions. The reason for pain is the reason for an alarm system, but many experiences of pain have side effects [Stevens & Grunan, 2005]. Many years ago, we knew that both the pain experiences provoked [Selye, 1974] ACTH response (alarm reaction), and, later, we knew that not only the ACTH but also the endorphin reaction is shared [Buchsbaum, 1982]. On the other hand, it is also well known that the physiological reaction that follows any painful experience is unspecific in the sense of being always the same whatever the painful experience is [Lyons, 1980]. All seems to point to the existence of a neurobiological defensive-protective mechanism that works whenever a dangerous signal is processed [Lazarus, 1966; Lyons, 1980; Horowitz, 1990].

Emotionally, painful feeling processing is sub-cortically and, therefore, unconsciously controlled by the temporal amygdala ordering all the body to response [LeDoux et al., 1984, 1986, 1990; LeDoux, 1995, 1996, 2000]. Not only the cardiocirculatory system, respiratory system, muscular system, and body language react, but also cognitively thinking neocortical neurons do. Strikingly, the experimental work we are referring to demonstrated that the cortex triggered his activity in response to an amygdala signal before knowing other information coming from thalamus without going through the amygdala filter [LeDoux 1995, 1996, 2000].

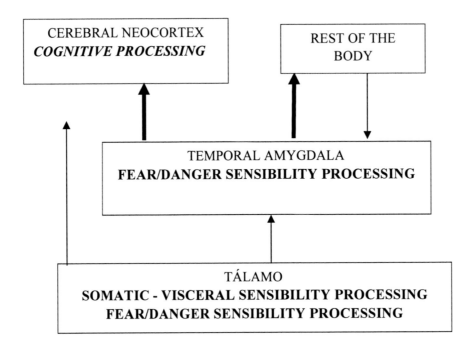

Heavy black line represents amygdala reaction.

Once the cortex received the delayed fearful information coming from the thalamus, the electrophysiologic activity of both the cortex and the amygdala did not change at all their electrophysiologic pattern of activity, which allows us to deduce not only that the cortex is not substantially influenced by the delayed information, but also that the cortex does not influence the amygdalar activity so triggered. As a concordant evidence, the experimental stimulation of certain nucleus of the amygdala is followed by a non-specific generalized activation of the cerebral cortex by means of the acetylcholine transmitter [Delini-Stula, 1991]. We can deduce the signal coming from the amygdala really conveys alarm or alert, but not any specific cognitive information [Kapp et al., 1992; Gallagher & Holland, 1994; LeDoux, 1995, 1996, 2000].

In sum, a brilliant animal experiment has allowed us to know the painful feeling-sensitivity processing pathways (LeDoux, 1995, 1996, 2000; LeDoux et al. 1984, 1986, 1990). This processing pathway has the primitive temporal amygdala as a control center that receives information from the thalamus. As soon as the amygdala codifies the signal as a danger, it triggers a response on to not only the cardiocirculatory system, respiratory system, and muscular system (body language included), but also cerebral neocortex that does not know the information unfiltered by the amygdala (the neocortex knows later).

This evidence represents a proof of functional connection between the feeling processing and the cognitive processing. The most striking fact is that when the cerebral cortex knows the information unfiltered by the amygdala, surprisingly the cerebral cortex does not change its ongoing bio-electrical activity triggered by the amygdala, which suggests the mental activity and its product, the thought, is that previously put in action on requesting of the amygdala. The whole process happens unconsciously. We will see the meaning of this concept later on. Even though assuming the limitations inherent to the extrapolation of animal experiment to human functioning, there is no reason, beyond any speculation, to think the human cortex works in different way.

At present, both the informative data-content processing [Das, 1999; Das et al., 1994, 1996, 2000] and the non-physical painful feeling sensitivity processing [LeDoux, 1995, 1996, 2000; LeDoux et al., 1984, 1986, 1990] have been neurologically explained according to powerful evidence. Years ago, evidence based on Claperade patient and patients suffering from interhemispheric disconnection allowed us to know that cognitive and feeling processing, although interconnected, could be dissociated [Gazzaniga & LeDoux, 1978; Sperry, 1983; Springer & Deutsch, 1988].

Since Claperade experience telling us that the intercommunication between one hemisphere and the other flows through deep areas of the brain in the absence of other connections, anatomic-physiologic studies have reinforced this knowledge [Guyton, 1971.p. 757; Guyton & Hall, 1996]. Later on, neurological unconscious cognitive-emotional processing evidence is quickly growing. Several fMRI studies have demonstrated conscious-deliberate processing activates cortical areas whereas unconscious-automatic processing does sub-cortical areas [Ojermann, 1976; Andreasen et al. 1995a, 1995b; ; Buckner et al. 1995; Tulving et al. 1996; Cabeza et al.1997; Jonides et al, 1998a, 1998b; Posner & Raichle, 1998; Smith et al, 1998; Cohen et al, 1999; Dolan & Fletcher, 1999; Dobbins et al., 2004; Sahrot et al. 2004]. Likewise, PET studies have revealed that a repetition task (priming) makes external cortical cerebral areas become less active (power cut) [Schacter et al. 1995; Blaxton et al. 1996; Schreurs et al. 1997]

Cortical brain activity is reduced when performing a repetitive task (neural priming). The human brain might rapidly circumvent deliberative processing in higher brain regions, called the cortex, as it learns to respond appropriately and automatically to stimuli such as repeated tasks. The brain is able to switch from one modality to the other. Particularly, a recent fMRI study consisting of presenting different faces with different emotional expressions to a blind individual showed that emotional expressions were identified, but faces not, which occurred with amygdala activation [Sahrot et al. 2004]. In any case, we count on fMRI evidence that impicit learning activates posterior brain, namely, parietal and occipital lobes, but not anterior brain, that is, prefrontal lobe [Rauch et al. 1997; Deckersbach et al. 2002].

According to our conception, what is highly relevant is the conclusion that our brains might cheat when learning or behaving, switching to 'automatic pilot' mode whenever it's possible. Instead of trying to answer a question by reasoning, our brain explores a catalog of previous answers to similar questions. The brain builds a repertoire of rote responses to frequently encountered problems that it can use as appropriate. This cheating mechanism also exists in people suffering from amnesia. This mechanism is highly efficient whether it is about learning or non-learning [Dobbins et al., 2004].

In normal condition, we can distinguish in EEG *beta (25-30 herzs/second), alpha 8-14 hz/s), theta(3-7 hz/s), and delta(1.5-2 hz/s)* waves. Each wave translates neural activation, therefore processing, and the absence of wave conveys neural rest. We also know different situations of information processing match different wave patterns and also it is assumed that the cerebral areas expressing the same wave pattern are part of the network processing the same information. *Beta* wave means maximum degree of information processing, which is associated with a maximum degree of asynchrony indicating many areas are involved in many different processing situations. *Delta* wave represents the opposite condition to *beta* wave. *Beta* and *alpha* wave are related to staying awake, *theta* wave to transition between wakefulness and sleep, and *delta* wave to sleep. We count on evidence that emotional stress may be associated with *theta* recording on EEG [Guyton, 1971. p. 759; Guyton & Hall, 1996], which is compatible with circumvention of the higher brain regions.

We must devote a brief commentary to unconscious feeling, which is, in fact, a paradoxical term because, by definition, pain is a conscious sensation. We can say that conscious pain corresponds to a clear discriminatory sensation, but subconscious non-clear discriminatory sensation in terms of comfort or discomfort also exists [Damasio 1994, 1995, 1999]. It is about something similar to the sensation we can perceive coming from the visceral system, for instance, the bowel system. In any case, subconscious feeling can be always observed in the reactive body response as we will explain later on.

We insisit that the most striking fact is that when the cerebral cortex knows the information unfiltered by the amygdala, surprisingly the cerebral cortex does not change its ongoing bio-electrical activity triggered by the amygdala, which suggests the mental activity and its product, thinking, is the same already previously in action on requesting of the amygdala [LeDoux 1995, 1996, 2000]. All this process happens unconsciously.

Keeping this in mind, we can neurologically explain that the cognitively thinking production of the cortex, operating under the order of the amygdala, is aimed not to stop the plan put in action in front of a life threatening condition. The cortex starts working and, as "a posteriori" action, it produces thinking that elaborates after processing the information entering the central nervous system coming from the external environment. When thinking activity happens, the thought produced is oriented to in real time explain or justify what that person can see, hear, touch, smell, and so on in the external scenery.

However, the body language response unconsciously triggered by the amygdala conveys painful feeling, although the conscious verbal language may say otherwise, denying bad feeling illogically. In fact, logically there is contradiction between arguments due to "a posteriori" neocortical information processing and body language expression due to amygdalar feeling processing. Cerebral neocortex does not receive cognitive informative data from the amygdala, but a physiological signal to be codified as a danger, which demands some kind of action. Depending on the magnitude of the painful-emotional sensitivity processed by the amygdala, related to both the memorized painful-emotional experiences in the past (identity) and the precipitating (triggering) experiences in the present (current precipitant factors), the painful feeling sensation will vary from unconscious to conscious level. In any case, body language will convey a painful feeling sensation.

Good logical reasoning as well as planning and decision-making fail when cognitive function is under the influence of bad feeling processing by the amygdala. Regarding this notion, the neurological evidence we count on is becoming overwhelming.

We count on neuro-physiological evidence of unconscious processing happening just before conscious decision making. The experiment of Benjamin Libet, neurophysiologist of California University, after the previous studies of German neurophysiologists HH Kornhuber and L Decke is astonishing [Degen, 2000, 2001; Libet, 1966, 1982], is astonishing. Individuals under experiment made decisions while under electroencephalography (EEG), electromyography (EMG), and the decision-making moment (will wave) being recorded. You can successively record EEG wave, will wave, and finally EMG wave during a period of one second, a period of time superior to what is needed for the neuronal signal to go from the neuron (EEG activity) to the muscle (EMG activity). Surprisingly, EEG wave appears before will wave with an unconscious period of time between EEG wave and will wave. Therefore an unconscious processing goes before the conscious processing of decision-making.

The second very striking point is the evidence that decision-making is determined by feeling, but not really rational thinking. More exactly, it is determined by feeling associated with thought or cognitive data content processed. In this respect, studies based on neurological lesions have been substantial [Damasio 1994, 1995, 1999]. The determinant reason for behavior seems to be feeling, but not knowledge. This can be to such extent that voluntary control (act of will) by the cognitive prefrontal cortex fails. For instance, any normal person behaves according to educational norms, it is said, because he/she has learnt (cognitive process) the norms, but clinical evidence of patients suffering from feeling-emotional prefrontal lesion (Damasio, 1994, 1995, 1999; Goldberg, 2001; Camille, 2004; Bechara, 2004) says otherwise. These patients behave against the educational norms because they do not feel badly, even though they rationally understand what they are doing. The experience with gambling games points to the same [Bechara et al. 1997, 2005].

In this view, the somatic marker hypothesis [Damasio 1994, 1995, 1999; Bechara et al.1997, 2005; Perez-Alvarez & Timoneda, 2007] is very reasonable. According to this assumption, the feeling phenomenon happens associated with vegetative, visceral, muscular, neuroendocrine, neurophysiologic activity that could be processed and memorized possibly at the right hemisphere according to neurological evidence.

Event Related Potential (ERP) is the evoked potential conveying the electrophysiologic activity of the neurons through the neurological areas involved in a circuit which is processing a stimulus entering via any sensorial input. This activity can be registered and assessed in terms of signal intensity (amplitude) and speed (latency) of transmission. The record displays a curvilinear graphic with positive waves (P waves) and negative waves (N waves). The P300 is, may be, the most well known wave. A longer latency of a individual in comparison with a control means a slower processing, which can be attributed to a dysfunction of circuits equal in length or, instead, to different circuits in length in one case and the other. It turns out that the amplitude of ERP in response to linguistic stimuli is higher in the left than right hemisphere and, instead, amplitude in response to non-linguistic stimuli (more linked to feeling) is higher in the right than left hemisphere [Molfese et al.,1975]. Non-linguistic stimuli are preferably processed in the right hemisphere. We know that the right hemisphere can codify non-linguistic information (body information) according to other sources of research. This gives plausibility to the somatic marker theory of Damasio [Damasio, 1994, 1995, 1999; Bechara et al. 1997; Bechara et al. 2005], which, in fact, links with the visceral feedback theory of James-Lange [James, 1890].

Likewise, we count on evidence that skin conductance activity precede the decision-making act [Bechara & Damasio, 1997; Bechara et al. 1997, 1999, 2000, 2005], which allows us to deduce that some kind of unconscious processing associated with somatic-visceral activity takes place before conscious decision-making happens. If so, we can assume that this previous unconscious processing influences conscious-declarative decision-making. Strikingly, the more painful consequence follows decision-making, the more intense is the skin conductance activity [Bechara, 2004; Bechara & Damasio, 1997; Bechara et al. 1997; 1999; 2000, 2005].

From human clinical evidence, years ago we knew that the decision-making process has to do with the prefrontal cortex [Stuss & Benson, 1986; Fuster, 1989]. Later, we knew that two prefrontal cortex can be differentiated-dissociated. One, the dorsolateral, the cognitive processor of data-content, and the other, the older medial-ventral prefrontal cortex, the feeling processor of the data-content being processed at any time.

Nevertheless, the more innovative concept was that the decision-making process involves two mental operations, one, the cognitive that allows us to rationally deliberate, and the other, the feeling operation associated with the cognitive operation. Moreover, the decision-making depends more on the feeling prefrontal activity than on the cognitive prefrontal activity in the sense that the more reasonable decision happens when the emotional prefrontal is intact, but not when it is not [Damasio, 1994, 1995, 1999].

Therefore, we must insist that human clinical evidence suggests that the decision-making process linked to the planning process, supposed to be exclusively dependent on cognitive deliberative prefrontal cortex, is nowadays thought to be dependent on feeling prefrontal cortex, which accounts for an individual with lesion in feeling prefrontal cortex, dorsolateral cortex being intact, to behave unsociably without remorse or, likewise, gamble without concern for the painful consequences [Damasio, 1994, 1995, 1999; Perez-Alvarez & Timoneda, 2005].

In sum, human clinical neurological evidence [Teuber, 1964; Luria, 1980; Stuss & Benson, 1986; Fuster, 1989; Thatcher, 1991, 1992] informed us that, indeed, planning [Das et al. 1996] depends on prefrontal cortex. On the base of lesion studies, later, [Damasio, 1994, 1995, 1999], it was stated that two dissociable prefrontal cortex could be differentiated-dissociated, namely, the external cognitive dorsolateral prefrontal cortex and the medial-ventral-inferior "emotional" prefrontal cortex in charge of processing the feeling-sensitivity of the data (informative cognitive content). This evidence, lastly, is convergent with the evidence reported by fMRI studies [Greene et al. 2001; Singer et al, 2004; Camille et al. 2004; Bechara, 2004; Perez-Alvarez et al. 2006c].

Relevant is also the neurological evidence that both the cognitive executive-planning processing and the feeling processing interact such that a dysfunction in one system determines a dysfunction in the other. For instance, the hypersensitive painful feeling processing determines a non-correct function of the planning. This feed-backed interaction [Sharot et al. 2004] can be initiated by any cause primarily acting at both the feeling network level and the planning network level [Goldberg, 2001].

The interaction cognition - feeling has been documented by MRI-based measurement of volume technique. Hippocampal (more related to cognitive processing) volume decreases in front of stress, but not amygdala (more linked to feeling processing) [Bremmer et al. 1995]. It has been also reported that chronic psychosocial stress causes apical dendriticatrophy of hippocampal CA3 pyramidal neurons in subordinate tree shrews [Magarinos et al. 1996].

Therefore, painful-sensitivity feeling and, equally, the subsequent impulse control [Hollander, 2001; Hollander et al. 2003] seems to be neurologically dependent on the balanced function of both planning processing and impulsive processing, such that any cause acting on either neurocircuitry can produce impulsive neurological activity with variable external behavioral expression. In other words, planning dysfunction activates painful feeling-impulsive processing and vice versa, painful feeling-impulsive dysfunction makes it difficult planning function [Goldberg, 2001].

In terms of neurological circuits, we can summarize that recent evidence in animals and old anatomical evidence and recent fMRI evidence in humans increasingly suggest that the painful feeling processing, in general, is supported by a network integrated by thalamus, amygdala, anterior and posterior cingulate cortex, insula, and anterior-ventral-medial prefrontal cortex, whereas the most external cortical structures, namely, dorsolateral prefrontal, temporal, parietal and occipital are responsible for the processing of concepts or ideas [Perez-Alvarez et al.2006]. We postulate that the interaction between these two neurological networks takes place according to the explanation we have discussed.

On account of didactic clarification, we will in short proceed to exemplify how what we are explaining in neurological terms can be described in behavioral terms. We will resort to two metaphors we usually utilize when applying the therapeutic procedure: the what-are-you-doing and six-month-old-baby metaphors.

The first metaphor deals with a 3-year-old child carrying some toys, his mother, and his mother's friend walking in single file. Suddenly, the little boy runs into something and noisily falls. He does not cry. On hearing the noise, the mother and the mother's friend turn around. The exaggeratedly scared and bodily frightened mother shouts: What's up? The little boy starts crying. Then the mother's friend asks: why does he cry? She answers: he ran into something.

Although all seems to make sense, apparently something is wrong. The little boy really cries due to his mother's shouting, but not to the fall. The mother's shouting happens as a non-reflexive unconscious overreactive-automatic behavior like a neurological reflex, presumably determined by the danger processing at amygdalar neurological level. Taking into account the little boy did not get hurt, the mother's behavior must be considered an overreacting behavior, a disproportional behavior in terms of cause-effect.. If so, her behavior must be considered basically a consequence of a highly over-sensitive felt internal condition (personal identity) coming from the experienced past, the little boy accident being just a triggering factor. When the mother is asked a question by her friend, her thinking brain, which is not at all responsible for the overreacting behavior, produces an answer.

According to extrapolating experimental neurological evidence [LeDoux 1995, 1996, 2000], the thinking brain produces an afterthought. In front of the question, it analyzes quickly what is entering her senses, that is, the experience taking place outside in real time. To elaborate the answer, the thinking brain resorts to previous accumulated - memorized knowledge. In this case, for instance, "a little boy who falls may be injured and subsequently cry". In other words, the thinking brain does not do anything that compromises the overreacting behavior triggered by the brain processing a danger signal.

The second metaphor has to do with a 6-month-old infant who is taken to my office by her parents and her grandmother. She is laid on my office table, her grandmother stands near the table, her parents sit down in front of me. Suddenly, the infant intends to sit up. Practically he can not get hurt. The grandmother does not move at all, but her father swiftly goes to the table and by using his hands helps the infant to sit up. Then, I ask him: what was up? He answers: he may fall.

Again this example shows overreacting behavior on the part of the father, the triggering factor, the over-sensitive internal condition that makes him process more fear than the situation deserves, and an answer in form of afterthought that is elaborated resorting to a memorized knowledge base.

Both metaphors are complemented with the following discourse: "I am wondering how the little boy and the infant will have memorized their experience. I am afraid that every time the little boy behaves doing something that provokes pain to his mother, his mother unconsciously triggered will overreact similarly as a consequence more of her past experience than of the immediate fact. If so, again and again this mother will be conveying (and the boy will be experiencing) a message we can formulate in terms of "you are unable / you do badly". This way, the "I am not able / I feel badly / I feel unconfident / I am guilty" may be building inside unconsciously. We must say that blame sentiment experience corresponds to the painful feeling processing associated with a cause - effect relationship where the person experiencing this sentiment processes "I am not doing well, correctly. I am responsible for",making the personal causal-effect responsibility into causal-effect culpability (moral guilt).

This unconscious-implicit mental process is happening continuously such that the experience of "doing wrong" tends to be implicitly processed as that of "doing morally wrong". This painful processing is extraordinarily devastating from the point of view of personal identity, sef-confidence, self-steem, and so on. Continuing with the example, I am afraid that every time the infant intends to do something by herself (sit up, walking, and so on) and memorize "I am able / I am confident / I feel well", her father, who is constantly seeing more danger than expected, will overreact overprotecting and preventing her from experiencing a confident-constructive belief".

Development is characterized by change or growth with increasing in complexity not only in the areas of motor and manipulative abilities but also in cognitive and emotional functions. Between 14 and 18 months of age, infants start understanding what the others want and also they tend to linguistically affirm their own will with the word "no" in their vocabulary. In fact, this developmental milestone shows the natural tendency of human beings toward an autonomic existence. The autonomic experience proves to be crucial for developing confidence against fear (painful feeling).

Other instances may be illustrative. A patient tells us: "Well, I am nervous and I get nervous easily. But children, traffic jams, my secretary, my boss. You know! " We can see that he totally justifies his behavior by finding a logical cause – effect explanation, resorting to immediate precipitating factors. However, if we find the markers, then we have the clues to diagnose a masked behavior. First, if we get more precise information on the alleged causal factors, then, perhaps, we will conclude we are in the presence of disproportional behavior (first marker). Second, our patient may not be accompanying his verbal irritation with a congruent body suffering (second marker: contradiction between body and verbal language). Third, our patient two days before does not behave similarly, although the same argued causal factors concur (third marker: verbal contradiction). We can distinguish precipitant causal factors from personal identity in the terms we have explained above.

Or someone may tell us "I hit him, he insulted me". If we inquire the nature of the insult, we'll see how disproportional the response was. Again, the second and third marker we have referred to above will probably be present in this case.

Another instance would be that surgeon who devotes more dedication than expected to his/her patient according to the nature of the operation. The disproportional dedication is well apparent at first sight. Someone can argue a "voluntary" over-dedication is laudable and worthy. Of course, this is true, but the matter is the difference between a pleasant over-dedication and an unpleasant one. And we must add not only pleasant but also non-compensating pleasant over-dedication. A behavior put in action to compensate for an unconscious badly unconfident feeling is first felt as a pleasant compensation. In other words, if I'm feeling unconfident, I have to behave to feel myself better (compensating behavior like, for instance, over-dedication). When the compensating behavior becomes insufficient, then the behavior is consciously felt; it is felt painfully. In psychotherapy terms, some cases need to get to this last described stage to be successfully helped. The second marker would be unpleasant body expression in contradiction with happy words. Even the third marker could be present in the sense that the reasons alleged to his over-dedication could sometimes be incongruent.

Before proceeding, we must insist on the concept of conscious pleasant compensating feeling associated with behavior put into action to compensate for unconscious painful-emotional feeling (lack of self-confidence), which is neurologically processed-codified as a danger signal. We must add that the pleasure of a pleasant compensating behavior is not that of a non-compensating behavior. This last one is like tranquility, relaxation, and peace that we can see in body language. As we have said, the personal unconfident feeling can be to a certain extent compensated for by means of compensating masked behaviors, but just to a certain extent; because beyond the conscious pleasant compensating behavior becomes conscious painful behavior.

The fact is that sometimes the painful feeling, neurologically codified as danger, is consciously experienced, but sometimes it is unconsciously-subconsciously experienced, although painful sensation is a linguistic term linked to consciousness. That is, the person behaving aggressively is not simultaneously aware of his/her conscious bad feeling (we call it rage), but he/she is unconsciously feeling badly and, in fact, the aggressive behavior should be considered a compensating reactive behavior to the bad feeling being unconsciously processed, which allows him/her to feel better, doing the behavior than not doing it. In this condition, the cognitive neocortex of this person is aware of the verbal or/and gesture aggressive behavior unconsciously triggered, but not of the real reason (painful feeling) responsible for it.

From a neurobiological point of view, we must insist that the sensitivity neurons responsible for the painful-emotional processing codify as a danger what we call pain, confidence or guilt / blame, among other different linguistic terms. Any experience of conscious pain, conscious confidence or conscious blame implies the painful-emotional processing is working. But, subconscious pain, subconscious confidence and subconscious blame are also possible and even more frequently possible. The above case of the surgeon is a clear example. In fact, subconscious danger processing is better diagnosed by looking at the behavioral reactions it brings about. Emotional subconscious feeling sensitivity is not neurobiologically different from non-discriminative propioceptive (muscular) or visceral sensitivity at physical level. But, we must remember that the psychological concept of personal identity regarding self-concept and self-esteem should be translated into basically unconscious self-confidence in terms of danger processing.

We have stressed throughout that a substantial component of a good logical reasoning has to do with the planning function [Das et al. 1996]. Only good logical reasoning allows us to plan any action, which basically implies the ability to foresee the consequences derived from the action. Years ago we knew executive function (something very similar to PASS planning function) had to do with the prefrontal lobe [Stuss, & Benson, 1986; Shallice, 1988; Fuster, 1989]. Has the achievement of the thinking cortex been an advantage? Has planning ability been an advantage? The automatic mechanism, in contrast to the thinking conscious attention mechanism, is simpler in both anatomy and function and works independently of conscious attention, resulting in faster performance. So far, the automatic mechanism is more efficient for quick action as in the case of a dangerous situation. For dangerous situations, being proficient on an unconscious level is a great advantage. However, planning ability allows us to learn to prevent dangerous consequences derived from the actions. However, again, we must remember that an efficiently operative planning depends on painful feeling processing.

AUTISM AS A CLINICAL MODEL

In this line of thought, regarding cognition - emotion interaction, autism represents an excellent clinical model. In fact, autism may be considered a clinical model of failure in executive function, but not in other cognitive functions (memory, for instance), associated with failure in emotional function. Strikingly, autistic children have more frequent than expected by chance a background of affective disorders [DeLong, 1999]. We must remark that studies conducted with high-functioning adults with autism or Asperger's syndrome highlight patterns of decreased activation in ventromedial prefrontal cortex, temporo-parietal junction, amygdala, and periamygdaloid cortex, along with aberrantly increased activation in primary sensory cortices [Di Martino & Castellanos, 2003].

From the point of view of cognitive function, we must remark that autistic children cognitively communicate by using body language (gesture), a less complex cognitive system than the cognitive system based on language. All the autistic behaviors can be accounted for such sd uncontrolled impulsivity plus failure in planning (executive dysfunction). Depression, anxiety or fear (they avoid the unknown) can be experienced by autistic children as an expression of feeling sensitivity in the sense we are dealing with. So autistic children really feel at least in the sense they experience these painful feeling behaviors. In other words, painful feeling processing seems to work properly. In fact, the paradigmatic and characteristic autistic behavior of failure in eye contact or/and lack of interest and /or non-participative attention / non-participative play may be understood as a prototypical flight behavior. Some characteristic behaviors related to emotion like affective indifference or the lack of feeling embarrassment where others feels it, and nonsense laugh may be interpreted as failure in understanding (planning that gives sense to the thought) followed secondly by failure in feeling. We consider the interacting mind theory must be understood in these terms [Frith & Frith, 1999]. Years ago, it was said that we can get to know by means of body language what the other person we are intercommunicating thinks, feels, and intends to do [Guilford, 1980].

Other behaviors like irritability, tantrum, rage, and aggresision can be understood as impulsive behaviors uncontrolled by the planning function. Likewise, the so-called obsessive - compulsive behavior, and bulimia as a compulsive eating disorder, may be considered a prototype of impulsive behavior without planning. But impulsive motor behavior without planning may be also considered hyperactivity, stereotypy as persistent repetition of an activity, iteration in manipulation of objects, and iterative routines. And the same meaning in verbal terms may be given to verborrhea and verbigeration or frequent and obssessional repetition of the same word, phrase, or even sound without reference to its meaning like, for instance, parrot speech.

IMPULSIVITY

We can make some progress towards discussing the notion of impulsivity in contrast to reasonable conscious control. What is it about? New developments in impulsivity have been recently reported [Hollander, 2001, Hollander et al., 2003]. Impulsivity, in particular attention deficit hyperactivity disorder, has been defined in terms of "the failure to resist an impulse, drive, or temptation that is harmful to oneself or others" [Hollander, 2001].

However, from a neurological point of view, impulsivity may be considered a linguistic term used to describe a concrete behavioral pattern characterized by what we call, in linguistic terms, "impatience, careless, risk-taking, sensation-seeking and pleasure-seeking, an under-estimated sense of harm, and extroversion". Any behavior occurs because of neurological processing. Then impulsivity takes place by means of neurological information processing. In fact, any behavior has both a somatic processing responsible for the locomotor component and a high level cognitive processing responsible for the thinking activity. On the other hand, it is evident that any behavior implies an integrated feeling processing in the sense of good feeling or bad feeling. So any behavior implies both a cognitive and a feeling component, as we do not get tired of saying again and again.

At present, the new knowledge concerning both the cognitive processing and the feeling processing represents a new understanding of impulsivity behavior. We may then assume that impulsivity behaviors are motor and verbal tic, stereotypy, compulsive behavior, hyperactivity, addictive behavior, and so on. The cognitive processing can be understood according to the PASS theory [Das et al. 1979, 1994; Das, 2003]. The PASS planning [Das et al.1996; Das, 2003] is a function similar to, but not equal to, the executive function of Fuster [Fuster, 1989] or frontal function of Stuss & Benson [Stuss & Benson, 1986] and has to do with the decision–making and impulse–control.

Since LeDoux [LeDoux, 1996, 2000], the feeling neurocircuitry in regard to bad feelings (fear / danger) has been described. LeDoux and coworkers have demonstrated how fear is unconsciously processed in such a way that the amygdala becomes the primary control center that shoots uncontrolled automatic defensive response as a security mechanism, which means that amygdala action is not controlled by neocortex action depending on the degree of fear processing. Either impulsivity or hyperactivity or aggressive behavior, indeed, can be considered different behavioral patterns of failure of impulse control and they have been experimentally reproduced.

The impulse control depends on a balanced function of both planning processing and fear processing, so any cause acting on either neurocircuitry can produce impulsivity. Furthermore, neurological evidence tells us that the nucleus accumbens, the anterior cingulated cortex, the ventro-medial prefrontal cortex, and the orbitofrontal cortex might play a role in control of impulsive behavior.

Addictive behavior to cocaine and amphetamine has been investigated in rats such that addictive behavior is considered a model of impulsive - compulsive behavior with failure of executive prefrontal control [Nestler, 2001]. There is evidence that this kind of addictive behavior is associated with prefrontal hypoactivity [Volkow & Fowler, 2000, Goldstein et al., 2001] just like in attention deficit hyperactive disorder [Zametkin et al., 1990]. So far, what we do not know is whether prefrontal failure is primary or secondary to impulsivity-feeling failure. An experimental fact we know is that a psychostimulant works by producing wakefulness, concentration, and other "side effects" like anorexia as a consequence of alert - alarm state. In the addictive state, deprivation is followed by fatigue, irritability, hyperactivity, tremor, anxiety, depression, and so on. Exactly, this constellation of manifestations match impulsive behaviors. In sum, this evidence has to do with the existence of a feed-back prefrontal - limbic system where the top - down control fails [Nestler, 2001].

Then, the next notion to remember again is that painful-sensitivity feeling is neurologically experienced in countless circumstances; we describe them with nearly countless linguistic terms, namely, anxiety, depression, stress, fear, anger, worry, uncertainty, fatigue and so on, but also in unthinkable circumstances like aggression, violence, and so on that we can include in the impulsive behavior category. Nowadays, many psychopathologic disorders like binge eating, personality disorder, maniac disorder, addiction, gambling addiction, kleptomaniac, ADHD, Gilles de la Tourette, schizophrenia, and autism are considered impulsivity disorders [Ros et al. 2002]. That is, painful-feeling processing provokes a reactive impulsive behavior (fight behavior), although the opposite can be also possible (flight behavior).

We will see that the painful feeling processing becomes equal to the impulsivity processing, this last term conveying the behavioral reaction in particular. Striking evidence from animal experimentation [LeDoux et al., 1984, 1986, 1990; LeDoux, 1996, 2000] suggests that the impulsive processing responsible for impulsive behavior is not different from the painful-fearful feeling processing we are talking about. That is, all evidence points to the conclusion that all live beings hold an anatomical-biochemical-physiological neurological mechanism in charge of processing countless situations or experiences that are codified as dangerous events. This is because the involved neurological structures are not able to discriminate the real danger from the unreal one on an evolutionary basis.

RESISTANCE AND TREATMENT

At this point, we will begin with a brief discussion of resistance. The more intense the painful-unconfident feeling is, the more resistant the masked protective defensive behavior is. This is a characteristic principle of behavioral dysfunction. We count on some neurological foundation for resistant behavior. Neurological evidence points to the fact that painful feeling processing is given top priority. From animal experimentation, we know that "neutral" repetitive stimuli make the cortical activation decrease in intensity, which we know as habituation to the stimulus. However, repetitive stimuli, making cerebral areas associated with reward-punishment be active, provoke increasing neural activity in the involved cortical areas as the stimulus is administered again and again. We call this phenomenon reinforcement, meaning that neurons are programmed to guarantee the memorization of the experiences linked to feeling processing [Guyton, 1971.pp.780; Guyton & Hall, 1996], greatly related to danger processing.

Furthermore, an inverse more-less response of cerebral areas involved in punishment and reward has been found. A repetitive stimulation of punishment areas determines a decreasing response to stimulation of reward areas. On the contrary, the stimulation of reward areas determines the same described effect on punishment areas, but to a lesser degree. So punishment processing is given priority to reward processing [Guyton, 1971.pp. 779; Guyton & Hall, 1996].

This evidence would allow us to postulate that an over-stimulation (extreme suffering) acting on the painful feeling processing center would be needed to defuse the protective response (masked behavior) in cases of highly resistance masked behavior. If so, compensating behaviors which provide pleasant compensation must disappear as a necessary condition to achieve success in therapy. That's why systemic therapy works [Minuchin, 1974; Madanes, 1985].This line of thought is in accordance with the principles of primal psychology. In the guideline chapter we will return to that.

Evidence extensively stated is that a conditioned behavior is not inextinguishable, but we know that the neuronal synaptic association involved in conditioning may at least partially persist even though the external conditioned behavior has disappeared. This is particularly true in the case of fear conditioning. The electric activity of neurons in the amygdala of rats was recorded. The activity and interactions of neurons increased spontaneously and in response to a fear conditioned stimulus, and, most important, some of the synapses created by conditioning did not disappear even though the external behavior had extinguished [Quirk et al. 1995]. This evidence helps us to explain the difficulty in solving some dysfunctional behaviors (resistance).

Also, we know that the inferior-medial-ventral prefrontal cortex plays a substantial role for the extinction of emotional learning [LeDoux 1996, 2000]. The experimental lesion of this prefrontal cortex in rats made these animals keep responding to a fear conditioned stimulus while other rats with the whole prefrontal extinguished the response [Morgan et al. 1993]. This evidence provides substantial knowledge on the role of the medial-ventral prefrontal in fearful feeling processing in accordance with the evidence from studies of humans with prefrontal lesions. This evidence supports the idea that the beliefs can be changed by transforming the feeling associated with the cognitive component of the beliefs.

HYPNOSIS

Now, it is useful to discuss briefly the point of hypnosis [Sugarman, 1996]. We should note that hypnosis, an important tool in our therapeutic procedure, is being understood in the light of neurology. Hypnosis is a well-known therapeutic procedure, but it is not clear why it works. Hypnotic suggestions are argued to be able to influence behavior when the listener is able to (a) be relaxed, receptive and open to the suggestions, (b) experience visual, auditory, and/or kinesthetic representations of the suggestions, and (c) anticipate and envision that these suggestions will result in future outcomes. As far as we know, however, nobody can satisfactorily explain why one individual can be helped, but another one is not. The answer to this question may be closer if we consider what we know at present about the mechanism of production of the human behaviors at the neurological level.

We know some interesting facts at the neurological level. Electric stimulation of particular thalamic areas related to attention activates specific zones of the brain cortex responsible for conscious processing, but not all the cortex in general when mesencephalon is electrically stimulated. This means that, under determined circumstances, wide cerebral areas involved in conscious thinking processing can be functionally excluded [Guyton,

1971.pp.757; Guyton & Hall, 1996]. This phenomenon is precisely inherent in focussing attention associated with hypnosis. Attention extremely focussed reduces the conscious span, which implies the exclusion of the neurons not involved in processing what is the focus of attention. This way, either pain or other thinking processing neurons different from those under the focus of attention do not work under hypnotic circumstances.

Therefore, hypnosis implies extreme focus of attention. Attention implies conscious activity. Conscious activity implies conscious reasoning and conscious feeling. By extremely focussing attention, conscious reasoning is unavoidably centered on what is under focus, and simultaneously conscious feeling is limited to what is under focus. This is the way hypnosis works. Ericksonian hypnosis is simply a kind of hypnosis.

According to our framework, hypnosis, in particular, Ericksonian hypnosis [Grinder et al. 1978; Erickson & Rossi, 1981; Watzlawick, 1985] works because it makes it possible the recipient of therapy to process a non-painful relaxing feeling, which contributes to avoid the resistance triggered by the painful feeling processing. In turn, this effect allows unmasked rational thinking to operate producing or facilitating a change in beliefs. As painful feeling beliefs are working when someone is suffering from any problem, a pure direct rational communication is not successful because it involves painful communication, instead hypnotic communication is an excellent resource because it does the opposite.

We'll remember the example according to which a child is asked to pronounce the successive combination "b, u, s", and he/she answers (output) correctly. Then, he/she is asked to pronounce the sequence "q, u, s", and the answer (output) is again /bus/. Incorrect answer. If we ask him/her: "How do you do it?" He/she will answer: "I did it this way", which is his/her conscious behavioral answer (external output). Frequently, the verbal answer is not in agreement with body language. In fact, the answer will be fabricated by his/her neocortex using the information in real time coming from the outside, that is, taking all the information entering via sensorial gates. Really, his/her unconsciously processed knowledge, that is, belief, not susceptible to be consciously and verbally reported, is the symbol "b" sounds /b / whether right side up or not. So the determinant reason for the behavior was the central unconscious belief. Only changing this belief the behavior will change consequently. Even to change this belief, apparently based on pure cognitive component, painful-feeling processing has to be taken into account. Ericksonian hypnosis has proved to be an excellent therapeutic tool to face painful feeling processing and the change of beliefs. This is usually the case in dyslexia patients.

We are saying, essentially, the hypnotic communication neurologically operates by extremely focussing attention. The attention extremely focussed involves that the thinking activity has necessarily to do with what is the focus of attention. What is on focus of attention is what is communicated or suggested, always both verbal and non-verbal content, to make the aimed effect. This has to be considered a necessary condition.

But we claim that this is only possible on the condition that the individual does not put in action defensive-protective-resistant behaviors triggered as a consequence of painful feeling processing [Lazarus, 1966; Lyons, 1980; Horowitz, 1990]. Only then, he/she will be able to focus his/her attention and to think to make a decision (to will) without the influence of bad feeling. We claim that the successful therapeutic effect happens when the person receiving therapy is able to process what (both cognitive and feeling message) we communicate by means of both verbal language and body language such that he/she can make a change in personal beliefs.

This change in personal beliefs requires a cognitive processing of concepts-ideas, but it is a necessary condition that the feeling processing happening on the therapeutic act be a good feeling processing, that is, an empathic act. To reach a successful hypnosis, in sum, the first condition is to reach a good feeling processing with the recipient of therapy. To reach the therapeutic effect, in turn, the condition is again the same. In sum, this is a concept of empathy based on neurological evidences of feeling processing.

Chapter 5

OUR RESEARCH

First of all, we have carried out the translation and factorial analysis validation of the DN:CAS battery in order to be used in Spanish and Catalan population [Das et al. 2000]. From the sample of validation study we extracted a normal control group (n = 300) we have been using in further studies.

We have learnt and reported [Das et al.2000] that technical instructions in applying the attention tests are crucial in order to obtain accurate results. Instructions must be clearly understood by the child given the test and who is giving the test has to be vigilant the child does not utilize some strategy like eye screening. We have been able to demonstrate that failure in this procedure can explain that planning and attention do not isolate in factor analysis.

We have found that the children who were administered the DN:CAS, whatever the reason (cognitive/learning or non-cognitive), showing underscoring (-1SD) in PASS processing more frequently showed mixed deficiencies rather than a single one in the following scheme: planning, attention, and successive tend to be associated in different ways, such that we have not seen isolated attention deficiency, but we have seen any combination of attention with planning and successive. The most frequently isolated deficiencies are planning or successive. An infrequent isolated deficiency we have seen is PASS simultaneous deficiency [Perez-Alvarez & Timoneda-Gallart, 2006. Assessment of Cognitive Processes: The Basis of Intelligent Behavior. In F Columbus (Ed.), *Psychological Tests and Testing.* Hauppauge, NY: Nova Science Publishers, Inc.]. The fact that simultaneous processing appears associated to any other processing less frequently than the rest of processes is in accordance with the neurological notion that simultaneous is supported by the posterior brain whereas the rest of processes are supported by the anterior brain.

Gifted children (n = 66) with behavioral problems scored under 85 (-1SD) in PASS planning (unpublished results) in a frequency higher than expected by chance when compared with a normal matched control group (n = 300) ($\chi^2 = 6.67$; $P < 0.01$). We must remark that DN:CAS measures planning, but other batteries do not, which must be taken into account [Perez-Alvarez & Timoneda, 2004b].

Timoneda-Gallart C & Perez-Alvarez F. (1994). Successive and simultaneous processing in preschool children. pp.156. Madrid: *Proceeding Book 23rd International Congress of Applied Psychology*.

We reported our first results on successive and simultaneous processing after applying K-ABC to a sample of 300 subjects. The two processes were clearly identified in the Hispanic population.

Perez-Alvarez F & Timoneda-Gallart C. (1998). *Neuropsicopedagogia. ¿Es como parece?*. Barcelona: Editorial Textos Universitarios Sant Jordi.

This book deals with the cognitive-emotional procedure we practiced since 1994. This procedure was later applied in practice on the occasion of two doctoral theses in the University of Girona {Mayoral-Rodríguez, 2002; Alabau-Bofill, 2003].

Perez-Alvarez F & Timoneda-Gallart C. (1999e). Dysphasia and dyslexia in the light of PASS theory. *Rev Neurol, 28*, 688-69.

Summary. *Introduction.* The PASS theory of intelligence understands the cognitive function as an information process or program that can be differentiated in planning, attention, successive and simultaneous. Every process is linked to an anatomical region: planning to frontal cortex, attention to frontal cortex and subcortical structures, successive to frontal cortex and non-frontal cortex and simultaneous to non-frontal cortex. Effective remediation is possible when a PASS pattern is known. *Objective.* To verify whether dysphasia and dyslexia [Das, 1998] have a typical PASS pattern. Material and method. The subjects were divided in three groups comprising 12 children with dysfasia, 12 children with dyslexia and 10 children with dysfasia and dyslexia, all of them between 6 years and 12 years of age, the majority boys. All children were administered the DN:CAS test to define the PASS pattern. A control group with 45 normal children was used. *Results.* Dysphasia shows poor successive and simultaneous process. Dyslexia shows poor successive process. The successive deficiency is poorer and in a different way in dyslexia than in dysphasia which is inferable from comparative analysis between groups. *Conclusion.* Dysphasia and dyslexia show a typical PASS pattern that allows an appropriate remedial training as a neurocognitive approach. The PASS diagnosis is a psychogenetic diagnosis which is different from the usual diagnosis based on semiology or results obtained with tests that explore non-PASS cognitive function.

The comparative analysis between groups was planned as follows. The aim was to establish differences in PASS processing between *dysphasia* and *dyslexia,* and between these well defined categories and those individuals with a combined *dysphesia-dyslexia* pattern. The design was according to the illustration that follows. The means were compared according to Student's t-test. As we have just said *dysphasia* shows dysfunction (processing under 1SD) in *successive* and *simultaneous* at significant statistical level. *Dyslexia* does it in *successive.* The differences between groups are illustrated in the next graphic.

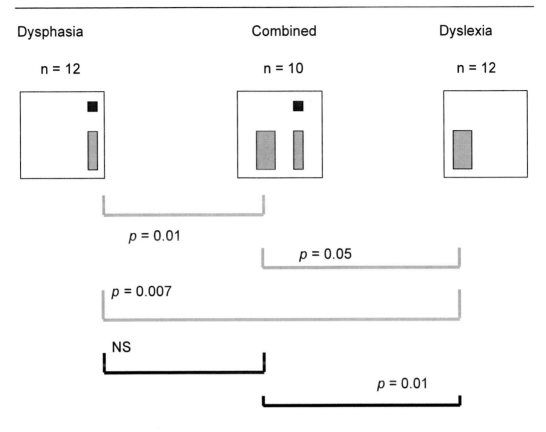

Black = simultaneous Gray = successive
Gray line = comparison in *successive*
Black line = comparison in *simultaneous*

As you can see, dysfunctional *successive* is present in the three groups. Dysfunctional *simultaneous* only in *dysphasia* and *combined* groups. The dysfunctional *simultaneous* in the *combined* group must be due to the *dysphasia component.* According to *p* values, the *successive dysfunction* is higher in *dyslexia* than in *dysphasia* and the *combined group* is more *dyslexic* than *dysphasic.*

Perez-Alvarez F & Timoneda-Gallart C (2000). Dyslexia as a dysfunction in successive processing. *Rev Neurol, 30,* **614-619.** *http://www.revneurol.com /3007/i070614.pdf.*

Summary. *Introduction* We present a study on reading and writing difficulties after normal instruction during a year [Rapin & Allen, 1983, 1988; Shaywitz et al. 1995; Shaywitz, 1998]. Focus: Verifying if these patients showed a specific pattern of PASS cognitive processing; if so, it allows us a rapid diagnosis and a useful cognitive remediation according to the PASS theory of intelligence. *Patients and method.* 30 patients were selected from neuropediatric patients because of learning disability. They were selected according to their performance on several tests of phonological awareness and a test of writing to discover errors in spelling. Patients with verbal language problems, as in dysphasia, and patients with learning difficulty not determined by reading or writing were ruled out. A control group of

300 scholars was used. The translated DN:CAS battery was administered to the study group and the control group for assessing the PASS cognitive processing. Statistical factorial analysis of the control group was performed as a validity confirmation to discriminate the four PASS cognitive processes. Cluster analysis of the study group was performed to discriminate its homogeneity. Differences between means were tested with the Student's t-test. *Results.* The four PASS cognitive processes were identified in the control group. The study group scored less than minus 1 SD in successive processing, the rest of the processes being clearly higher than minus 1SD, and the mean of study group was inferior to control group (P= 0.001). *Discussion and conclusions.* A kind of dyslexia may be defined by dysfunction in PASS successive processing.

Das JP, Garrido MA, Gonzalez M, Timoneda C, Pérez-Álvarez F. (2000). *Dislexia y dificultades de lectura.* **Barcelona: Paidós Editorial.**

We have translated to Spanish the book Das JP (1998) Dyslexia & Reading difficulties. Edmonton, Canada: University of Alberta. Apart from the translation, we have written a chapter summarizing our results on PASS theory of intelligence linked to feeling processing.

Perez-Alvarez F, Fàbregas-Alcaire M, Timoneda-Gallart C. (2007). Dyslexia, phonemic and acoustic processing. *Rev Neurol* **(in press).**

Summary. *Introduction.* Developmental dyslexia has been explained to suffer temporal [Galaburda, 1993; Tallal, 1980; Tallal et al. 1993] and, mainly, phonemic processing dysfunction as well as cognitive dysfunction. *Objective.* To test whether temporal, phonemic, and cognitive processing are interrelated. *Patients and methods.* After medical screening, 36 subjects, 7 to 14 years-old, boy/girl ratio of 2:1, were selected with phonemic processing tests. For every subject, two normal controls were also selected with the same phonemic tests. DN:CAS cognitive battery for diagnosing of cognitive processing was administered to subjects, and both subjects and controls were examined with a temporal processing test, made in a laboratory, consisting of two kinds of items, syllables with a transition period of 40 milliseconds and other longer ones. Proportions and means were statistically analyzed. Factorial analysis was applied to scores in DN:CAS and syllabic acoustic tests. Results. The dyslexics, compared to controls, made more errors in the acoustic test ($z = 6.73$; $p < 0.000$). The DN:CAS mean obtained by the dyslexics was lower than controls ($t = 6.73$; $p = 0.001$). The factorial analysis accounting for 77% of the variance identified the acoustic test as a sequential processing test. *Conclusions.* On the basis of the cognitive psychology of information processing and neuroscience, arguments are exposed to suggest that phonemic, temporal, and cognitive processing may be different expressions of the same central neurological mechanism. This conception implies therapeutic considerations in the sense that dysfunctional reading can be trained without reading material. On the other hand, the acoustic test is suggested as a useful test to screen dyslexic children.

Table. Factorial analysis DN:CAS + acoustic test

	Factor 1 Attention	Factor 2 Successive + Acoustic test	Factor 3 Planning	Factor 4 Simultaneous
Acoustic test	21895	58134	09375	28103
Attention				
ATT_G	81882	17171	30931	01208
ATT_EA	52883	07318	23828	02211
ATT_RA	82188	13217	12883	01135
ATT_NF	71283	07282	22438	12871
Planning				
PLN_G	33298	10236	73232	18312
PLN_VS	27383	05237	78383	23371
PLN_MN	22208	19121	62288	22832
PLN_PC	28323	08372	83486	18234
Successive				
SCC_G	14223	98862	13282	21833
SCC_NR	28283	73548	15488	18575
SCC_WO	17882	68257	08733	13323
SCC_SRQ	08227	82342	12211	21438
Simultaneous				
SMT_G	23238	28226	22423	82317
SMT_FM	28113	13133	18213	62823
SMT_MA	08282	05412	12233	85283
SMT_SV	18541	22838	11332	88354

Perez-Alvarez F & Timoneda-Gallart C (2007) Assessment of Cognitive Processes: The Basis of Intelligent Behavior. In F Columbus (Ed.), *Psychological Tests and Testing.* **Hauppauge, NY: Nova Science Publishers, Inc. (in press).**

Further studies on language, reading, writing, and learning are on course [Vilanova et al. 2003].

Perez-Alvarez F & Timoneda-Gallart C. (1999c). The hyperkinetic child in the light of PASS theory. *Rev Neurol, 28*, **472-475.**

Summary. Introduction The PASS theory of intelligence is a new conception of the cognitive mental function. According to this theory, we think we learn by using four programs or processes: planning, attention, successive and simultaneous. We can assess every process as an entity. Every process is linked to an anatomical region: planning to frontal cortex, attention to frontal cortex and subcortical structures, successive and simultaneous to no-frontal cortex. This relationship between program and specific anatomical region does not mean every program does not use different non specific anatomical regions. *Objective.* To verify whether the patients with attentional deficit disorder and hyperactivity and impulsivity show a characteristic pattern of information processing according to PASS theory. *Material and method.* A group of 33 patients with attentional deficit disorder with hyperactivity and impulsivity, selected according to DSM-IV criteria, was compared to a control group of 45 normal subjects. The DN:CAS battery was used. *Results.* The patients with attentional deficit disorder showed more frequently worse planning ($P=0.001$). Furthermore, worse attention ($P=0.05$) and worse successive ($P=0.05$). Also, they showed more frequently ($P=0.001$) the association planning-attention-successive in deficient way. *Conclusion.* The basic problem in attentional deficit disorder of this kind is planning. The concurrent deficit in successive and attention supports the hypothesis of failure in the frontal cortex, concretely, in the control unit. This would explain, also, the impulsivity.

Perez-Alvarez F & Timoneda-Gallart C. (2001). Neurocognitive dysfunction in attention deficit disorder. *Rev Neurol, 32*, **30-37. http://www.revneurol.com/3201/k010030.pdf**

Summary. Introduction Attention deficit disorder shows both cognitive and behavioral patterns. *Objective.* To determine a particular PASS pattern in order to early diagnosis and remediation according to PASS theory. *Patients and method.* 80 patients were selected from the neuropediatric attendance, aged 6 to 12 years old, 55 boys and 25 girls. Inclusion criteria were inattention, 80 cases, and inattention with hyperactive symptoms, 40 cases, according to DSM-IV[DSM-IV 2000]. Exclusion criteria were the criteria of phonologic awareness previously reported, considered useful to diagnose dyslexia. A control group of 300 individuals, aged 5 to 12 years old, was used, criteria above mentioned being controlled. *Procedure.* DN:CAS battery, translated to native language, was given to assess PASS cognitive processes. Results were analyzed with cluster analysis and Student's t-test. Statistical factor analysis of the control group had previously identified the four PASS processes, planning, attention, successive and simultaneous. *Results.* The dendrogram of the cluster analysis discriminated three categories of attention deficit disorder. First, the most frequent, with planning deficit. Second, without planning deficit but with deficit in other processes. Third, just only a few cases, without cognitive processing deficit. Cognitive deficiency in terms of means of scores was statistically significant when compared to control group ($P=0.001$). Discussion and conclusions. According to PASS pattern, planning deficiency is a relevant factor. Neurological planning is not exactly the same than neurological executive function. The behavioral pattern is mainly linked to planning deficiency, but also to other PASS processing deficits and even to no processing deficit.

Table. *Cluster analysis* **showing PASS profile distribution in ADHD**

Groups	N	Sub – Groups	N	dysfunctional	PASS	profile
	Total	ADHD-C	ADHD-I			
1	52	33	19	1.1	35	P + A + Su
				1.2	9	P + A
				1.3	6	P + Su
				1.4	1	P + Si
				1.5	1	P
2	20	5	15	2.1	12	Su + A
				2.2	4	Su + Si
				2.3	2	Si
				2.4	2	Su
3	8	2	6			
	n = 80	n = 40	n = 40		n = 80	

P= planning A= attention Su= successive Si= simultaneous. ADHD-C = combined type ADHD-I = inattentive type. Dysfunctional PASS processing was considered a processing equal to or inferior to 1 SD according to DN:CAS manual. All these cases with processing equal to or inferior to -1SD were also equal to or inferior to -1 SD when compared with controls. Furthermore, the *mean* value of the study group and the three groups, 1, 2 and 3, was inferior to the control *mean* (p <.001). You can see isolated dysfunction of *attention* does not appear, nor does *attention-simultaneous* association..

Our research on attention deficit hyperactive disorder has been set out in the following publications:

Perez-Alvarez F & Timoneda-Gallart C.(2004a). Learning Both in Attention Deficit Disorder and Dyslexia in the light of PASS Neurocognitive Dysfunction. In HD Tobias (Ed.), *Focus on Dyslexia Research.* **pp. 173-179. Hauppauge, NY: Nova Science Publishers, Inc.**

Perez-Alvarez F & Timoneda-Gallart C.(2004b). Attention Deficit / Hyperactive Disorder as Impulsivity Disorder according to PASS Neurocognitive Function. In P. Larimer (Ed.), *Attention Deficit Hyperactivity Disorder Research Developments.* **pp 173-184. Hauppauge, NY: Nova Science Publishers, Inc.**

We show here what we consider a remarkable fact concerning DN:CAS assessment versus other different tests, in particular, WISC-R. As you can see WISC-R does not assess planning. We have observed, for instance, that many children who score as gifted children in WISC-R have dysfunctional planning in DN:CAS assessment.

Table. Factorial Analysis WISC-R + DN:CAS (n=60)

	Planning	Attention	Successive	Simultaneous	¿?
DN:CAS					
Planning	.812	.128	.256	.114	.103
Matching Numbers	.886	.345	.307	-.011	.129
Planned Connections	.642	.247	.164	.238	.072
Attention	.021	.879	.191	.154	.294
Expressive Attention	.211	.747	.409	-.010	.304
Number Finding	.132	.730	-.123	.305	.187
Successive	.245	.253	.895	.149	.243
Word Recall	.346	.306	.866	.134	.148
Sentence Repetition	.131	.128	.808	.126	.307
Simultaneous	.098	.148	.131	.917	.063
Matrices	.046	.037	.126	.848	.079
Simultaneous Verbal	.212	.174	.024	.730	.021
WISC-R					
Verbal IQ	.267	.270	.117	.258	.908
Information	-.015	-.001	.082	.153	.836
Similarities	.212	.220	.200	.083	.819
Vocabulary	.227	.247	.205	.067	.833
Arithmetic	.236	.369	-.220	.515	.437
Comprehension	.286	.268	.205	.183	.584
Digit Span	.335	.388	.639	.088	.212
Performance IQ	.368	.359	.284	.741	.347
Picture Completion	-.035	-.028	.329	.187	.668
Picture Arrangement	.039	.030	.162	.701	.228
Block Design	.327	.300	.350	.554	.170
Object Assembly	.118	.090	-.077	.852	.191
Coding	.401	.763	.313	.311	.065

Pérez-Alvarez F., Timoneda-Gallart C., Font X., Mayoral S. (1999). Inteligencia PASS y Síndrome de Williams. *Rev Neurol 28* (Supl.), 201.

It is frequently reported that Williams syndrome patients have different kinds of dysfunctional processing. In particular, dysfunctional spatial processing has been reported again and again. In PASS terms, we can affirm a global dysfunction is observed in these patients.

Pérez-Álvarez F & Timoneda-Gallart C. (2005). Intellectual function: what is it about? *Acta Pediatr Esp, 63*,101-4.

Summary. Introduction. Intellectual function is not clearly defined so far in neurological terms. Since 1994, we count on a conception based on neurological evidences, the PASS theory that refers to the four programs: planning, attention, simultaneous and successive. *Objective.* To verify if the WISC-R cognitive battery assesses the cognitive PASS function and, in particular, the planning, the most valuable program on intellectual basis and the program most susceptible to be treated, if needed. *Patients and method*. 60 normally scholar children were selected, aged 5 to 12 years old, 30 boys and 30 girls. Procedure. WISC-R and DN:CAS, translated and validated battery for assessing PASS processing, were administered. Results. The four PASS processing, planning, attention, successive and simultaneous, were identified by factorial analysis and also the correspondence between PASS processing and the tests of WISC-R was established. The tests of WISC-R mainly assess PASS simultaneous processing and somewhat successive and attention. No test of WISC-R identifies PASS planning processing. *Discussion and conclusions.* The PASS concept is explained with particular emphasis on the planning and its relationship with the so-called executive function. From both diagnostic and therapeutic point of view, it is claimed as an advantage to be able to assess intellectual capacity as a neurological mechanism of production by means of non – heterogeneous and specific tests that can be used by pediatricians devoted to both the developmental and the social field. We insist on the dynamic conception of intelligence this knowledge implies, which allows us to suggest a redefinition of the mental retarded category.

Pérez-Alvarez F, Timoneda-Gallart C. (1996). Epilepsia y aprendizaje. *Rev Neurol, 24,* **825-828.**

This report deals with cerebral processing in terms of simultaneous and successive processing in a sample of 33 epileptic children at ages 3 to 12 years. Epileptic children with idiopathic or cryptogenic epilepsy were selected according to the following criteria: two clinical seizures with convulsive movements, with unconsciousness, with no fever, with focus in intercritical EEG and normal brain scanner. All of them attended ordinary school. A sample of 261 normal children was used as a control group. The K-ABC battery was administered to both epileptic and control group. The results were analyzed in terms of Student's t-test, 2 test, stratified 2 test, and factor analysis. It is concluded that a kind of epilepsy may be associated with poorer performance in successive processing.

Factorial analysis of epiléptic children (N = 33).

K - ABC test	Factor 1 Successive	Factor 2 Simultaneous
Gestalt	0.320	**0.608**
Triangles	**0.557**	**0.568**
Matrix	0.018	**0.849**
Spatial memory	0.294	**0.740**
Pictures series	**0.746**	0.385
Word series	**0.846**	0.132
Hand movement	**0.693**	0.351
Number recall	**0.828**	0.109
% total variance	51.5	13.6

Perez-Alvarez F, Timoneda C, Baus J.(2006a) Topiramate and epilepsy in the light of DN:CAS, Das-Naglieri Cognitive Assessment System. *Rev Neurol, 42,* **3-7.**

Summary. *Introduction.* Cognitive side effect is a possible effect of topiramate. Cognitive function is not unanimously defined and a test measures according to what the concept is based on. On the other hand, behavioral dysfunction is frequent in epileptics and the euthimic effect of topiramate on impulsive dysfunction is known. *Objective.* To assess the cognitive effect of topiramate with a modern battery, DN:CAS, which diagnoses mental programs, but not only achievement. Also, to test the influence of topiramate on behavior. *Patients and methods.* As a prospective study, 35 patients with idiopathic or cryptogenic epilepsies were administered DN:CAS battery, and, simultaneously, patients and parents were given behavioral questionnaires at baseline, and after 6 and 12 months on topiramate. Cognitive scores were compared to those of a group of healthy controls at baseline, and baseline scores were compared to 6 and 12 month follow-up scores within the patient group. Student's t-test was applied. *Results.* Patient scores were lower in successive processing before treatment as compared to controls (P < 0.001). After 6 months no change was noted. After 12 months of treatment, patients scored significantly better in planning processing than before treatment (P = 0.04) and, moreover, improved behavioral scores were noted. *Conclusions.* The patients showed a successive processing dysfunction not related with topiramate. An improved planning processing and behavioral pattern were observed 12 months after treatment. According to the euthimic effect of topiramate and the neurocognitive - neuroimpulsive interaction, a positive effect of topiramate on DN:CAS cognition and behavior can be postulated.

Table. DN:CAS assessment of epileptics before treatment (n = 35)

PASS: CAS	Epileptic subjects before treatment(n = 35)			Control(n = 324)			
	N	Media	DS	N	Media	DS	*p*
Planning	35	94.66	11.72	324	97.73	13.33	NS
Attention	35	93.73	10.19	324	96.34	16.02	NS
Simultaneous	35	102.27	12.81	324	105.89	12.91	NS
Successive	35	83.95	11.14	324	93.76	15.78	.001[*]

* Student's t-test: 3. 64

Perez-Alvarez F & Timoneda-Gallart C. (2002). Emotional behaviors as a neurological dysfunction. *Rev Neurol,* **35, 612-624. http://www.revneurol.com/LinkOut/form MedLine.asp?Refer=2001110**

Summary. Introduction. The hypothesis that the emotional component of behaviors can be explained by a specific neurological mechanism was stated. *Patients and method.* A sample of 749 cases, all between 5 and 14 year old, with different behavioral and cognitive problems was selected from attendance to the Neuropediatric / Neurobehavioral Unit from 1994 to 2000. A sub – sample of 20 cases with PASS planning processing scoring less than 1SD was also selected. A design of mainly qualitative research according to case analysis was followed, behavioral data being provided by patients and their parents and analyzed with video recorder assistance. To avoid bias in the study, techniques such as triangulation were applied. Quantitative cognitive data were obtained by using DN:CAS battery for diagnosis of PASS processing. A procedure for diagnosis and treatment of behaviors, previously reported, was followed. The cases of the sub – sample were tested before and after emotional treatment without cognitive remediation, the results being tested by Student's t-test. *Results.* The responders were 82% according to not only the criterion of solution of the behavioral problem, for example, anorexia, psychosomatism, non – neurological paroxysm and so on, but also, the sufficient amelioration assessed by the patients, their parents and the researchers. All cases, however, required the disappearance of observable defensive behaviors in enough quantity to deduce an important maturation change. Significant difference was observed in planning. *Discussion.* Defensive behaviors as masquerade behaviors are explained in the light of neurological reasons. The neurological processing of the "sensibility" of danger is emphasized according to the most recent knowledge. *Conclusion.* All behaviors can activate the neurological processing of danger feeling.

Concerning quantitative investigation, we tried to verify the interrelationship between cognition and emotion when we designed the following study. We selected two pre and post treatment groups. One group was only emotionally treated. The other was only cognitively treated. As you can see, both groups responded with improvement in planning, but strikingly although the cognitively treated group improved in planning and simultaneous, the emotionally treated group improved in planning at a higher statistical level of significance. You can also see this in Perez-Alvarez & Timoneda-Gallart (2006) Assessment of Cognitive Processes: The Basis of Intelligent Behavior. In F Columbus (Ed.), *Psychological Tests and Testing.* Hauppage, NY: Nova Science Publishers, Inc..

Table. DN:CAS assessment before and after only PREP cognitive intervention[*]

	Before PREP	After PREP	
	n σ SD	n σ SD	t P[**]
Planning	35 81.5 13.4	35 89.1 11.4	2.6 0.047
Attention	35 88.3 14.3	35 90.3 13.3	0.7 NS
Simultaneous	35 86.3 13.5	35 94.0 14.5	3.0 0.029
Successive	35 79.8 08.6	35 80.8 11.3	2.7 NS

[*]Das (1999b) PREP: *PASS Reading Enhancement Program.* Deal, NY: Sarka Educational Resources.
[**] *"p"* values Student's t-test, paired samples.

Next, we show the DN:CAS results after only emotional intervention:

Table. PASS assessment before and after only emotional intervention[*]

PASS processing	Pre-Test			Re-test			
	n	Mean	SD	n	Mean	SD	p**
Planning	20	83.90	11.24	20	89.65	13.38	.008
Attention	20	92.95	15.17	20	95.15	15.02	NS
Simultan.	20	86.15	14.31	20	88.35	13.56	NS
Successive	20	88.75	13.03	20	92.50	15.35	NS

* Perez-Alvarez & Timoneda (1998). Neuropsicopedagogia. ¿Es como parece?. Barcelona: Editorial Textos Universitarios Sant Jordi.
** "p" values Student's t-test, paired samples.

After the publication of these results, we obtained similar results with a larger sample (n = 60).

Concerning qualitative investigation, we must emphasize the following results:

The therapeutic procedure is basically based on indirect both verbal and non-verbal communication such as metaphor, amnesia post-trance, indirect question, introductory phrases and included phrases on the discourse, ambiguous terms, saturation of channels of information, melodramatic expression, or confusion in any way, paradox, silence, dissociation, hypothetical phrases, false alternative option, prescription of the symptom, and such. We concluded that these techniques make effect promoting a non-painful feeling processing, which is accomplished by getting an extreme attention focalization (trance state in hypnotic terms). In this state, the mental thinking of the patient receiving the communicative therapy has to be devoted to necessarily process what is being communicated, but not to think (to process rational argued reasons) against it due to the painful feeling processing as we will explain in the next section.

Countless experiences were identified as precipitant-triggering causal factors. We identified the behaviors as behavioral patterns that we classified into DSM-IV categories as we show in the next tables. Countless concrete behaviors were identified as masked painful-feeling-emotional behaviors according to the criteria we will expose later in the next section.

Table. DSM-IV diagnostic approach

Diagnosis	N
Learning problem	144
Only communication problem (language)	91
Stuttering	14
Attention deficit disorder with / without hyperactivity	96
Selective mutism	7
Conduct disorder [a]	107
Anorexia / Binge eating disorder	106
Enuresis / Encopresis	79
Tics[b]	24
Depression	81
Anxiety	236
Somatization	348
Total	1333

[a] Conduct disorder: It includes, among others, oppositional defiant disorder, asocial – aggressive behavior, bullying, teasing, and intimidation, drug abuse.
[b]Tourette disorder excluded.

Table. Somatization disorders

Somatization disorders	N
Cephalalgia	179
Pseudo - epilepsy	16
Ataxia	4
Paralysis	4
Amblyopia	3
Anosmia	2
Dizziness / Faintness	11
Asthma	10
Abdominalgia	119
Total	348

Reinforcement-resistance of masked painful-feeling-emotional behaviors was consistently observed in response to any therapeutic intervention communicating in such a way that the recipient of the therapy would process painful feeling as the conceptual framework predicts.

The personal belief processing, the real reason for putting in action the masked painful behaviors, was inferred according to the following scheme that we will explain in the Guideline chapter:

DIAGNOSIS				INTERVENTION
Behavior **He/she says** + **He/she does**	Belief **A** *is / is not* B	Personal Belief **Identity** *I can't... / I feel incapable* *I feel insecure* *I feel badly* *I feel guilty*	Pain	
1	2	3	4	

1. "Look, I'm very nervous. You know, my children are so naughty. Furthermore, the traffic jam is unbearable. I can't stand it any longer! On the other hand, my secretary is getting worse and worse, and my boss is becoming lunatic". - He talks with strong words and provocative gesture; his face reflects anger.
2. Being nervous is constitutional / Naughty children provoke nervous state. / traffic jam causes nervous state / And so on.
3. *I can't / I feel insecure / I feel badly / I feel guilty* if I'm not nervous and a series of factors or situations cause my nervous behavior. Whenever one processes *"I feel badly"* associated with a behavior, simultaneously one processes *cause-effect relationship badly.* We call this feeling badly *blame sentiment.* This sentiment may be either unconsciously or consciously processed, depending on the efficacy of the compensating behavior.
4. Body and paraverbal language expressing unpleasant sensation.

DIAGNOSIS	INTERVENTION			
	Behavior I say + I do	Belief A *is / is not* B	Personal Belief Identity *I can.../ I'm capable* *I feel secure* *I feel well* *Versus* *I can't / I feel incapable* *I feel insecure* *I feel badly*	Pain
	1	2	3	4

1. Look, it is amazing! I remember what happened to me years ago. Someone phoned me and asked me: "I would like to invite you to a conference on ... We have thought you could talk about .... ", in fact, a theme I was very familiar with. Do you know what happened? I looked at my agenda with concern. If my agenda was full, I relaxed and I apologized to him/her. However, do you know what happened otherwise? I didn't agree immediately. In fact, I tried finding some excuse, I believed it, to apologize and avoid the situation. Really, do you know why? I felt insecure, I was suffering just thinking I was going to assume that compromise. Next, I change the discourse to produce amnesia post-trance.

2. What we do is not always what we are / What we see as a cause is not always the real cause of the behavior.
3. *I can / I feel secure, confident / I feel well versus I can't / I feel badly /I feel insecure/ I feel guilty.* 4. Pacing.

According to this conception, we identified precipitant causal factors we show in the next table:

Table. Events appearing as significant precipitants factors

1. Family related:

- Death (father / mother, grandfather / grandmother,
  brother / sister friend, boyfriend / girlfriend)
- Family rows / Family violence
- Separation/Divorce/loving relationship breaking-off
- Birth of a new brother / sister
- Home departure
- Teenager pregnancy
- Disease (father / mother or other family member)
- Toxicomania
- Alcoholism
- Abuse
- Mother starting working
- Labor dismissal
- Move of house

2. School related:

- Starting schooling
- Move of school
- Change in teacher
- Problem with teacher

We concluded that all behaviors can be at least partially explained according to personal beliefs, which makes it possible to be able to explain the "order" and the "disorder" by a common mechanism of production (Power, & Dalgleish, 1997). Moreover, that the determinant reason for any behavior is the feeling component of the belief, but not the cognitive component.

Practically all the indirect verbal communication techniques were considered to work by promoting the focalization of the attention. This is the case, for instance, for: metaphor, amnesia post-trance, indirect question, introductory phrases and inserted phrases, ambiguous terms, saturation of channels of information, melodramatic expression, or confusion in any way, paradox, silence, and so on.

Certain indirect verbal communication techniques, in particular, dissociation, that is, the use of the first name of the patient instead of "you", hypothetical terms like "perhaps", "may be", "would ...", false alternative option linguistic formulation like "...and Joseph will do it before or after …?" and, mainly, the prescription of the symptom have a powerful effect on non-painful feeling processing. In particular, verbal and body pacing proved to be highly effective in this sense. Pacing consists of not fighting verbally and/or bodily against the reactive resistant masked painful behaviors. In general, the indirect communication techniques and, in particular, the metaphor as a prototype proved to be excellent resources.

The Ericksonian hypnosis technique involves a discourse formulated with ambiguous terms, undirected questions, introductory and inserted phrases, saturation of channels, confusion, silence, dissociation and so on, all of which induces both focalization and non-painful feeling processing (tranquility, relaxation in muscular terms). The para-verbally emphasized linguistic terms produce anchorage or analogic underlining effect. This means that an association between the cognitively processed informative content of the message and the simultaneous non-painful feeling is produced. Reinforcement of resistance-masked painful-feeling-emotional behaviors was consistently observed in response to any therapeutic intervention communicating painful feeling. We argue that the therapeutic procedure works because it causes an effect on a psycho-neurological mechanism of production of behaviors predicted by the conceptual framework.

Perez-Alvarez F & Timoneda-Gallart C (1999). Cognition, emotion and behavior. *Rev Neurol, 29*, 26-33.

***Summary**. Introduction.* We present neuropsicosomatic disorders diagnosed and treated during the period 1994- 1997. *Material and method.* A total of 83 cases, 24 boys and 59 girls, were selected according to suspected diagnosis. Their ages were in relationship with the psychosomatic disorder. These 83 cases are 10% of neuropediatric assistance in the period. A protocol was designed for disclosing any organic pathology. The method is based on the PASS theory of intelligence and emotion processing theory of masked behavior. The success was defined after a period of, at least, two years of follow-up. *Results.* Cefalalgia was the most frequent diagnosis. Language and learning difficulties, attention deficit disorder and pseudo-epilepsy were also frequent. Other diagnoses were: amblyopia, paralysis, pseudo-autism, tic, sphincter disorder, vertigo, mutism and sleep disorder. *Discussion.* Concerning differential diagnosis, it must be emphasized that complex partial epilepsy of frontal lobe can mimic psychosomatic disorder as short, less than 1 minute, automatism. Partial epilepsy of temporal lobe may also mimic psychosomatic disorder but epilepsy does not respond to psycopedagogic remediation. Tumor and migraine must be also disclosed in case of cefalalgia but they do not respond to psycopedagogic remediation. Neurological scientific bases of emotion processing theory are widely explained. *Conclusion.* Cognition and emotion are functions of the CNS so they are competency of neuropediatrician. On the other hand, it is convenient for neuropediatrician to know about behavioral analysis in order to improve diagnosis and economical cost.

Perez-Alvarez F & Timoneda-Gallart C. (1999). Behavioral phenotypes: cognitive and emotional rationale. *Rev Neurol, 29*, 1153-1159.

***Summary.** Introduction.* We present a series of behavioral phenotypes treated with neurocognitive and neuroemotional procedure. *Patients and method.* A sample of 26 cases were selected according to qualitative methodology from neuropediatric patients. The method was based in using the PASS theory of intelligence to approach the cognitive problem and the theory of masquerade behavior as self-defense to solve the emotional problem. Both theories have neurological bases. DN:CAS battery was utilized for assessment of cognitive processes. On the other hand, analysis of cases was carried out doing data analysis with video recorder device. *Results.* All cases were considered responder cases although to a different degree. The responder was defined as the patient which reached better intellectual achievement with respect to cognitive function and which gave up, at least partially, masquerade behavior with respect to emotional function. *Discussion.* The behavior of the behavioral phenotypes has neurological rationale. The PASS theory and the planning, in particular, supported by prefrontal cortex justifies consistently some behaviors. The masked behavior theory is explained by the fear emotional response mechanism which means emotion is a cerebral processing with neurological rationale. *Conclusion.* The behavioral phenotypes are behaviors and every behavior can be explained by neurological reasons both cognitive and emotional reasons. So, they can be treated by a cognitive and emotional procedure understood in the light of the neurology.

Perez-Alvarez F & Timoneda-Gallart C (2007) Assessment of Cognitive Processes: The Basis of Intelligent Behavior. In F Columbus (Ed.), *Psychological Tests and Testing.* Hauppuage, NY: Nova Science Publishers, Inc. (in press).

Summary. *Introduction.* The neurological foundation of both cognitive and emotional phenomenon has not yet been conclusively defined. However, nobody denies the interactive functioning of cognition and emotion. Understanding this interaction involves the understanding of behavior on a neurological basis. Both cognition and emotion, internal processes, can be assessed by means of external behavioral expression. Since 1994, we have counted on the PASS theory of intelligence, and since 1980s we learned part of painful emotional-feeling processing. From a holistic perspective, we have integrated both concepts to explain, at least partially, the reason of intelligent behavior in both a normal condition and a dysfunctional condition. *Method.* Since 1994, we conducted a line of research based on this framework, using both quantitative and qualitative method. *Results.* Our results have to do with normal and non-normal subjects. We have translated and factor-analysis validated the DN:CAS battery for assessing PASS processing (*P*lanning, *A*ttention, *S*imultaneous, *S*uccessive). In general, we have concluded that mixed processing deficits are more frequently found than single ones. We have defined characteristic DN:CAS profiles in dyslexia, attention deficit hyperactive disorder, and childhood benign epilepsy. Likewise, the profile of vulnerable gifted children. Of particular relevance is the finding of a DN:CAS profile related to dysfunctional emotional behavior, which means that a cognitive profile can be used to determine a cognitive dysfunction secondary to emotional dysfunction. Furthermore, we have established the relationship between planning and emotional processing, using functional magnetic resonance image methodology. A significant success rate in dysfunctional emotional behaviors has been accomplished by using a procedure based on the cognitive-emotional concept mentioned. *Discussion and Conclusions.* Neurobiologically speaking, behavior must be considered any body expression, whether verbal or non-verbal. In this sense, any behavior fulfills the PASS processing principle that says input, neurological central processing, and output must be differentiated. So, intelligent behavior is what we directly can observe, but the neurological central processing, non-directly observable, is what we must diagnose and treat. Beyond any concrete behavior, which we can call it, gifted child, dyslexic, ADHD, epileptic, dissocial behavior and so on, there is always a neurological central mechanism based on both cognitive and painful emotional-feeling processing, that is, both the cognitive component and the feeling-sensitive component of personal beliefs memorized all during one's life. The PASS mental operations, put in action to process any information entering the central nervous system, account for the personal beliefs. The main conclusion is that this conception has proved to be useful to diagnose and treat any dysfunctional intelligent behavior.

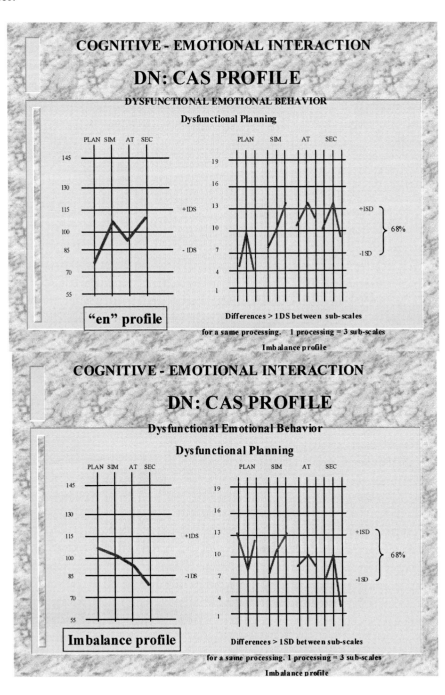

We have seen that planning underscoring (-1SD) in emotional behavioral disorders (n = 1333) is more frequent than expected by chance (χ^2 = 7.00; *P= 0.008*) when compared with a normal control group (n = 300). Moreover, we have identified a typical profile we call it "en" profile because the pattern is similar to the "en" letter, the frequency of which (n = 603)in children with emotional disorder is higher than expected (χ^2 = 8.00; *P= 0.005*) by chance, compared with a normal control group (n = 300). This profile is due to the fact that planning and attention, in this turn, are the most sensitive processes to emotional disturbances. This profile is associated with the fact that the sub-scales (each scale has three sub-scales) show differences between them superior to 1 SD. We must remember that emotional behavioral disorder, according to our concept, is defined as any dysfunctional behavior reactive to painful-feeling. Although the "en" profile is very characteristic, however any profile showing differences in score between subscales superior to 1 SD is suggestive of dysfunctional emotional behavior. We call it "imbalance" profile. This "imbalance" profile (n = 397) compared with a normal control group (n = 300) shows a higher frequency at significant statistical level (χ^2 = 6.64 ; *P=0.01)* In fact, there is no cognitive reasonable argument to justify differences higher than 1 SD in three subscales that are assessing the same cognitive entity.

Perez-Alvarez F, Timoneda C, Reixach J. (2006). An fMRI study of emotional engagement in decision-making. *Transaction Advanced Research*, 2, 45-51.

Regarding fMRI study, it has been suggested that decision making (planning) depends on sensitive feeling associated with cognitive processing rather than on cognitive processing alone. From human lesions, we know the medial anterior inferior ventral prefrontal cortex processes the sensitivity associated with cognitive processing, it being essentially responsible for decision making (planning). In this fMRI (functional magnetic resonance) study 15 subjects were analyzed using moral dilemmas as probes to investigate the neural basis for painful-emotional sensitivity associated with decision making. We found that a network comprising the posterior and anterior cingulate (classic limbic structures) and the anterior medial prefrontal cortex was significantly and specifically activated by painful moral dilemmas, but not by non-painful dilemmas. These findings provide new evidence that the cingulate and anterior medial prefrontal are involved in processing painful emotional sensibility, in particular, when decision making takes place. We speculate that decision making (planning) has a cognitive component processed by cognitive brain areas and a sensitivity component processed by emotional brain areas. The structures activated suggest that decision making depends on painful emotional feeling processing rather than cognitive processing when painful feeling processing happens. In psycho-educational words, this fMRI study tells us that cognitive performance depends on emotional state, when painful feeling processing occurs. In fMRI language, this finding makes plausible emotional mental block that we assume we can unveil as in "en" DN:CAS profile or "imbalance" DN:CAS profile.

Our fMRI study has allowed us to count on a fMRI normal pattern we are now comparing with different dysfunctional situations like, for instance, attention deficit hyperactive disorder. We have hypothesized that these children will show a different pattern from normal children, susceptible to be correlated with DN:CAS profiles.

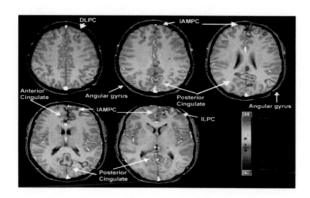

fMRI technique shows those cerebral areas that are significantly at statistical level working in comparison with the rest of the brain when the individual is doing any activity whether physical or mental.

This way, we can identify cerebral areas involved in a particular task or activity. This means we can interpret what is equal and what different in neurological terms

Figure 1. DLPC: Dorso Lateral Prefrontal Cortex; IAMPC: Inferior Anterior Medial Prefrontal Cortex; ILPC: Inferior Lateral Prefrontal Cortex

We designed an fMRI study aimed to dissociate the painful-emotional prefrontal network from the cognitive network and to support that decision making depends on the emotional rather than on the cognitive prefrontal cortex. Six males and nine females between 12 and 15 years of age, who were provided with written informed consent forms, were recruited from the local academic community. A medical screening was carried out to rule out any psychiatric or neurological illness or any medical condition or medication. All subjects were healthy and right-handed with average or above-average intelligence (WISC-III-R).

The stimuli selected were dilemmas. These were divided into "emotional" and "non-emotional" categories according to both their nature and the responses of 30 pilot participants. No emotional dilemma was felt emotional for one person and non-emotional for another. The emotional dilemmas involve a painful experience (blame sentiment) whatever the decision. Two options (A and B) are possible. Option A and B are painful, although one of them is the most painful. The selected non-emotional dilemmas are painless.

We assume that "emotional dilemma" is emotionally engaging, which means an intensively badly felt (blame) sentiment depending on the decision making response. Blame sentiment is an experience involving painful-feeling sensitivity, although other different processes may be also operating.

Testing materials were similar to those available online at www.sciencemag.org/cgi /content/full / 293/ 5537/2105/DC1.

Distinguishing between cognitive and emotional tasks can be argued as somewhat arbitrary for some cognitive component is always present. For this reason we are talking in terms of more or less a predominant cognitive component. To minimize the cognitive requirement we used a quasi-passive viewing procedure, which reduces the linguistic cognitive component of the task to a minimum. This makes comparison between cognitive and emotional condition much easier.

The task consists of viewing a picture (cartoon) that represents a selected emotional or non-emotional dilemma. Every dilemma had to have a "yes" / "no" response option with the minimal motion of the 1st or 2nd finger of the hand. As a previous instruction, the subjects were presented pictures similar to those used during the session. Once the task was understood, the subjects were presented a visual display with each dilemma in the form of a picture or cartoon.

Alternating blocks of emotional and non-emotional dilemmas were presented in random order in a series of three blocks of ten trials each. Every participant responded to each dilemma while undergoing brain scanning by fMRI. Stimuli were projected onto a white screen located in front of the child and automatically displayed for 5 s by means of a computerized system. A previous pilot study showed that this presentation rate allowed subjects to comfortably look at the picture and respond to it. Longer time on task tends to increase the involvement of cognitive network. The intertrial interval (ITI) lasted long enough to allow the hemodynamic response to return to baseline after each trial. During the ITI, participants viewed a fixation cross.

As we can see in the figure above, the whole brain analysis, performed to identify brain regions that showed greater activity for emotional dilemmas, showed that emotional dilemma condition had increased activity in a number of brain regions. The most statistically significant activation was in the posterior cingulate (BA 23/30/31). Other significantly activated regions included the anterior cingulate (BA 24/25/32) and medial anterior inferior-ventral prefrontal (BA 10/11). These areas were not significantly activated in a non-emotional condition.

In contrast, the dorsolateral prefrontal, angular gyrus, several regions of frontal, parietal and temporal cortex were significantly more activated during the non-emotional condition. This cerebral network is in accordance with what has been previously reported on ventro-medial prefrontal [Camille et al. 2004] and anterior cingulate [Damasio, 1999; Peyron et al. 2000] and also recently reported [Patel et al. 2005]. In particular, hypoactivity of dorsolateral prefrontal associated with hyperactivity of ventrolateral prefrontal and anterior cingulate has been reported in a study including 22 subjects suffering from obsessive compulsive disorder, which is considered an impulsive disorder [Ros, 2002].

In sum, the decision-making act linked to emotional feeling happens associated with the activation of cerebral areas different from those areas that activate when the decision-making act is not associated with painful feeling processing.

Perez-Alvarez F, Luque A, Peñas A. (2006c). Bilateral disc drusen as an important differential diagnosis of pseudotumor cerebri. *Brain Development* **(in press).**

Perez-Alvarez F, Mayol Ll, Luque A, Peña A. (2006e). Pseudohypoparathyroidism, movement disorder, and non-organic disease. *J Neurol Neurosurg Ps.* **URL:** *http://jnnp.bmjjournals.com/cgi/eletters/68/2/207*

These two reports are examples of how a psychosomatism can be associated to an organic pathology non-directly related to the psychosomatism.

Perez-Alvarez F, Peñas A, Bergada A, Mayol Ll. (2006d). Obsessive-compulsive disorder and acute traumatic brain. Acta Psychiatr Scand, 114, 295.

This report deals with our personal experience on a clinical model of impulsive behavior associated with medial-inferior-ventral prefrontal injury (Bechara, 2004). An 11-year-old boy was attended because of head trauma. There was no loss of consciousness but simply a brief period of dazed consciousness. In the emergency room, the Glasgow Coma Scale was 13. Confusion with amnesia (posttraumatic amnesia) was present for a few minutes. He had no focal signs, although in the immediate post-traumatic period he was ataxic. Neuroimaging study showed an MRI right medial orbitofrontal lesion with increased signal on T2. From the day of the accident to 3 days later, compulsions, aggressive intermittent explosive behavior, anxiety, panic, and depression appeared dramatically. Furthermore, he complained of poor concentration, forgetfulness, and sleep-wake disturbances. He was tested and performed badly on attention, memory, and complex executive tasks.

The MRI lesion disappeared after 12 weeks. This change can be interpreted as representing regional edema without contusion or infarction. The time course of the clinical recovery takes days only in the most trivial injuries but takes weeks to months in the more typical concussion. The symptoms of our patient disappeared gradually in accordance with the lesion evolution.

Chapter 6

GUIDELINE

Several different terms have been coined to design different conditions: Minor Neurological Dysfunction (MND), Soft Neurological Signs, Non-verbal Learning Dysfunction, Developmental Coordination Disorder (DCD), Obsessive Compulsive Disorder (OCD), and so on. Likewise, Specific Language Impairment (SLI) or Developmental Language Disorder (DLD) or Developmental Language Impairment (DLI), are all used for the old term dysphasia [Rapin & Allen, 1983, 1988; Shaywitz et al. 1995; Shaywitz, 1998]. And, on the other hand, the Attention Deficit Hyperactive Disorder (Barkley, 1997, 1998) is differentiated from similar condition like the Deficit in Attention, Motor Control and Perception (DAMP) [Gillberg, 1983]. Meanwhile, in 1995, the use of Ritalin ® increased by 250% and by 1997, that number reached 700%. Furthermore, in the year 2000, it was stated that 1 in 6 children in the U.S. suffered from autism, ADHD, aggression, or dyslexia.

The key question is diagnoses such as "learning disabilities", "disadvantaged children", "slow learners", "low achievers", "mentally handicapped", "behavior-disordered", and so on do not suggest a clear or specific course of remedial treatment. They may be useful for screening and classification, but not for diagnostic instrument and effective diagnosis going beyond categorizing children. It is easy to attach a very sticky label once you find it. In addition, these general labels may be frightening or prejudicial, giving the impression that the child cannot be helped. Intervention is possible although it is not about thinking but experiencing.

The fact is we are used to tons of theory and little practicality. Every day we confront theoretical discussions that lead nowhere. It is about the real nuts and bolts of teaching and helping children and persons in general. The study of how things work, on the idea that even the best you can find can probably be improved and/or combined with more of the best from somewhere else.

A point that we would emphasize once again is that even though reasoning is needed to communicate, however any successful treatment necessarily requires, first of all, to resolve the responsible bad feeling condition. In contrast, any action or procedure causing bad feeling will reinforce the masked painful-emotional behaviors, which will make it more difficult for success.

Long ago, it was established that cognitive performance, but not emotional "performance", is susceptible to be assessed and remediated, although it was likewise assumed that the emotional state influences the cognitive performance. The results of our research allow us to conclude that the practical procedure we utilize based on the theoretical framework already discussed is a useful one to diagnose and treat cognitive - emotional dysfunctions [Perez-Alvarez & Timoneda, 1998; Mayoral-Rodríguez, 2002; Alabau-Bofill, 2003].

The procedure has two components, the diagnosis and the treatment, simultaneously taking place and focussing on two basic mechanisms responsible for any behavior, one the cognition and the other the emotion in the sense of fearful-painful sensitivity feeling.

From the point of view of practical application, we we'll focus first on cognitive training and then on dysfunctional behavior treatment, although only didactic reasons justify this separate consideration.

THE COGNITIVE APPROACH

Let's proceed to discuss the cognitive training. First of all, we must say that an emotional intervention without using instructional cognitive material is practically always needed in those cases where a learning problem is paradoxically the principal concern, for instance, dyslexia (Alabau-Bofill, 2003).

From the point of view of our framework, emotional intervention involves the diagnosis of masked behaviors as a response to an unconfident-fearful-painful identity on the one hand, and therapeutic remediation on the other, oriented to transform an unconfident identity into a confident one. This change of personal internal sensitivity is affordable by achieving a change in beliefs and personal relationships [Minuchin, 1974; Madanes, 1985].

To reach this objective, we have verified the successful utility of indirect communication technique. Only a good logical reasoning allows us both to make decisions and to plan any action, which basically implies to foresee and feel the consequences derived from the action, and take the best option [Stuss & Benson, 1986; Fuster, 1989; Damasio, 1994, 1995, 1999; Das et al. 1996; Goldberg, 2001]. Otherwise, a masked planning lets us make masked decisions.

As we will see, the educator or therapist acts as a mediator but not as a instructor in the sense that the decision of changing is on the part of the patient. The educator is a mediator facilitating indirect inductive learning. Inductive learning has a double effect, cognitive and emotional.

As to PASS cognitive treatment, the first condition is to be able to diagnose the masked behavior, which conveys fearful-painful feeling. Planning processing is the PASS cognitive process more frequently deteriorated by the influence of emotional state. To master this aspect of the therapy, the interpretation of body language is essential as well as the diagnosis of personal beliefs.

Secondly, we must be able to diagnose cognitive strategies, which are really beliefs. Once an inefficient strategy is diagnosed, the therapeutic aim of the educator will be to change it into a more efficient strategy. To achieve this objective, we practice inductive learning by means of tutored-mediated training and furthermore indirect communication technique.

Inductive learning [Das, 1999b, 2003; Das et al. 1994, 1996, 2000] deserves a more extensive comment. We practice the inductive learning in our cognitive training by means of tutored-mediated intervention. Later on, we will extend the role of educator or trainer as mediator. It is well known that inductive learning has a more powerful memorizing effect than deductive learning. The inductive learning effect is not only cognitive but also emotional because this kind of learning is experienced and, at least, unconsciously processed and memorized, as "I know I can". This is recorded as an autonomic capability, that is, personal identity. In other words, it means self-esteem. Even though unconsciously, in fact, the learning of "I know I can" is a personal belief. The "I know I can" is simultaneously felt as "I feel confident and subsequently fine". The cognitive and emotional therapeutic effect is based on discovering personal beliefs and changing them by means of inductive learning and indirect communication and, in particular, the metaphor [Grinder et al. 1978; Erickson & Rossi, 1981; Watzlawick, 1985] as a prototype of indirect communication. The therapeutic effect is conveyed by means of both the verbal language and the body language, this one being a priority. The golden rule is communicating what we want to communicate without conveying painful feeling.

Unconstructive beliefs determine defensive - protective behaviors [Balmes, 1968; Goleman, 1986; Perez-Alvarez & Timoneda-Gallart 1998;Shand, 2000; Mayoral-Rodríguez, 2002; Alabau-Bofill, 2003] that must be understood by educators. Again, for the case of academic learning, teachers frequently admonish children not to respond quickly without thinking by saying "don't just guess". Children may take these words to mean that giving an exact answer is not acceptable. For a case of computing by estimating, they may be afraid of ridicule, and then they pursue computing the exact answer, when they are asked to estimate. Or a child is questioned by the teacher and a covering up behavior may be produced, for instance, mumbling to maintain outward appearance (belief: smart kids always answer correctly). Or, perhaps, the answer is not known and the child raises hand in response to teacher's question (belief: smart kids answer quickly). Or, anyway, any cover story when error is discovered. We must remark that any protective behavior is a short-term advantage and a long-term disadvantage. To discover these unconstructive beliefs is quite crucial to be successful in remediation.

At this point, we want to exemplify how the mental mechanism responsible for masked behavior in the context of dysfunctional behavior works also in the behavior of learning. We mean that the three markers that are characteristic of masked behavior, we have already explained another section, may be present here. In particular, the contradiction between verbal language and body language is very frequently observed. It goes without saying that body language is more reliable than verbal language. For example, "Bob, please, tell me about it. How did you do it? – " Hmm… let's see. Well, I did it…". He unconsciously moves his eyes up and to the left or to the right accessing visual PASS simultaneous processing. Or, maybe, level and to the right or to the left accessing auditory PASS successive processing. We can see verbal conscious explanation, if any, is not coherent (contradiction) with the movement of the eyes (body language).

The diagnosis of strategies is a key question for any teaching-remediation task. This diagnosis is set up since the very moment we contact the child. For instance, we can ask him/her a few questions to determine exactly what kind of eye movements are characteristic of him/her. We can ask what color the house is. Then the car, bedroom walls, and so forth. We'll see how he/she looks just before answering. Then we can ask him/her about some of his/her favorite songs and how they sound to her/him. We'll see his/her eyes just prior to the answer. Later, the DN:CAS administration will give us more information in this respect. The diagnosis of strategies involves looking for accessing cues like the eyes up and to the lateral position, for instance, that allows us to know simultaneous processing is working, or the scanning eyes that tells us planning is working. Likewise, repeated verbal or sub - vocal rehearsal to facilitate remembering tells us successive is working. We administer the DN:CAS to all patients regardless the motive of assistance.

We will remember how strategies (beliefs) must be diagnosed to correctly assess behavioral responses, and subsequently to plan our therapeutical intervention on both learning and behavior. Remember the instance of a child who is presented with single separated letters, concretely, u, b, s. He/she is asked to pronounce the successive combination b, u, s, and he/she answers correctly. Later, he/she is asked to pronounce the sequence q, u, s, and the answer is also /b u s/. Apparently, an incorrect answer was given. However, if the mentally processed knowledge is the symbol "b" independently of placing it right side up or not, then good logical reasoning has happened, because "a chair remains a chair whether its feet are on the floor or pointing toward the ceiling". For the child in the example to be able to learn further, it will be necessary for the educator, the therapist, to know this.

The DN:CAS produces a quantitative measure but, first of all, a current qualitative profile susceptible to be changed in the future. This means a dynamic concept of intelligence. This concept is advantageous in front of the old measure of IQ. A particular underscoring PASS process may be a consequence of primary innate reason. That may be true, in particular, in successive processing. A particular profile, like "n" and "unbalanced" profiles, may suggest to us a cognitive dysfunction secondary to emotional reason. Underachieving in learning performance may be because learning is carried out by using a learnt processing where other unlearnt processing will work out better. So, guidance for intervention is obtained when a particular profile is known. It is about using the best personal processing to solve any particular task of learning. In general, the cognitive training is oriented to minimize successive demand and maximize simultaneous application, which must be accomplished by the planning. Concretely, the planning training effect is achieved by making the child be conscious of the inefficient strategy and then making him/her be conscious of a new more efficient one that he/she will memorize.

We can say this procedure has to do with learning to learn by instrumental enrichment [Feuerstein, 1983] and metacognition practicing with educator being a mediator [Bruner, 1966; Vygotsky, 1978] rather than an instructor. Planning training aims to substitute an inefficient for an efficient strategy by means of inductive learning and indirect communication, and resorting to the previous concrete informal knowledge or zones of proximal development [Vigotsky, 1978]. We must consider a training program successful when not only near transfer but also far transfer happens, which has been verified in PASS planning training [Das..planning..]. Regarding guided discovery learning (tutoring), therefore, it is important to determine how and why, that is, the process by which a child arrived at an answer, the strategy the child employed to solve the problem [Bruner, 1966; Das et al. 1996, 2000].

The teacher or educator acts as an intermediary, that is, someone who helps external factors and internal factors to mesh in order to create opportunities for the child to discover. Children discover or are helped to find out thinking strategies, that is, thinking to himself/herself to figure out unknown combinations. The educator acts as hypothesis maker and hypothesis tester. Children need to be supervised so that a particular child receives guidance and correction when needed by means of "passive" techniques based on questions and demonstrations, and non-direct instruction. Verbal direct instruction may become a verbal act without meaning. Words need to be backed with actions, experiences actively involving children in a concrete representation ("empirical verification"). In fact, the aim is to unlearn the incorrect procedure and to learn the correct procedure later. This method is linked to procedure flexibility supported by planning that operates by choosing (decision making) the more efficient strategy that involves both speed and accuracy in performance, but not only speed. Children are not merely imitating adults but are struggling to construct their own system of rules. Guided discovery learning helps children to discover a relationship. Learning involves building upon previous knowledge, so the concrete informal experience-knowledge plays a key role in the meaningful learning of formal knowledge.

The mediator procedure can be summarized in three steps. Aiming the child to consciously discover the inefficient strategy, one first question must be formulated: How did Jordi do it? We use the called dissociation technique in indirect communication based on avoiding a direct reference with "you". Instead, "you" is substituted for the name. We will return on this technique later on. Frequently, the educator will have to help with hints indirectly. Second step will be a second question: How could/can we do it? Again, the formulation with "we" instead of "you". At this point, we are intending him/her to discover the new efficient strategy. This process of inductive "metacognitive" learning involves him/her to experience the "I'm able / I'm worthy / I feel very well" as expression of personal autonomy and decision-making, put aside the specific cognitive effect.

Indeed, it is well known that inductive learning has a more powerful memorizing effect than deductive learning. After a reasonable time without success, the educator – therapist will mediate, making some procedure without direct instruction. The aim is he/she be aware of a possible strategy to be put in practice. Direct verbal instruction is the least desirable method, because it is difficult to describe a mental procedure and instead explanations may serve only to confuse children.

Above all, do not pursue the matter. It may only frustrate the child, who may eventually discover the strategy later anyway. We must remark that any strategy to be indirectly induced has to meet the principle according to which any new concept to be learned by anyone has to be incorporated and related to his/her previous base of acquired knowledge,. And don't forget that concrete but not abstract concepts must be utilized. It is about creating opportunities for the child to discover a general rule. This is true, also, for building the personal beliefs.

So doing, not only near transfer linked to the context of learning but also far transfer (beyond the context of a particular learning) of strategies has been demonstrated [Das et al. 1994, 1996, 2000]. The far transfer involves the internalization of a principle or rule applicable to multiple contexts, it producing not only an immediate effect but also a sustainable effect.

We must remember that rote memorization, reinforced by repetition, is not comprehension. Meaningful knowledge happens by learning relationships and forming associations and comparisons (PASS simultaneous), which is inherent to memorization laws for long-term memory as it is the case in chunking, space-time contiguity, acrostics and acronyms, "sing-song" learning, etc. Successive is needed in a similar way to working memory [Baddeley & Hitch, 1974; Petrides, 1994; Van den Heuvel, 2005]. Planning allows us the maximal efficiency in simultaneous with the successive available. Attention is always working to allow us a conscious operation.

When the second step fails in reaching its objective, it is applied to the next step. The third step, the less efficient, has to do with a demonstration of a possible useful strategy. In extreme cases, direct intervention guidance may be necessary for learning mental procedure, but if it does not work, do not pursue the matter because it does not correspond to their informal notion. It may only confuse the child, who may eventually discover the strategy later anyway.

However, don't forget the role of explicit instruction must be understood as the educator may have to provide hints or help make the pattern explicit by modeling the task and "thinking out loud", and describing the procedure and rationale with verbal-explicit instruction associated with activities that involve a concrete representation. For instance, a child may need explicit instruction to learn the cardinality rule (how many things are counted). "After counting, I just repeat the last number I say. How may fingers do I have up? Let me count to see. 1,2,3,4. The last number I said was 4, so I have 4 fingers up."

Children will, without direct instruction, abandon concrete procedure and invent mental procedure. It may be that they could not retain the relationship until they see a meaningful connection with their experience. Children rely on their own invented procedures (planning) and tend to use their own resources. Self-invented procedures are more meaningful to a child whereas direct instruction is the least desirable method to describe a mental procedure so that explanations may serve only to confuse. It is about creating opportunities for self-discovery.

Next, we must remark that the PASS cognitive intervention is oriented to train the central neurological processing but not the resulting external product as it is the response to a task or a specific behavior. Although the behavior happening at the intake and output of information processing is used to both diagnose and treat, however the intake and output of information are neither diagnosed nor trained. This notion explains that we can cognitively train a dyslexic patient without using reading material successfully [Das, 1998; Das et al. 2000] or an ADHD case without focussing on attentional behavior [Perez-Alvarez & Timoneda-Gallart 1998; Mayoral-Rodríguez, 2002; Alabau-Bofill, 2003; Das et al. 2000], because the behavior is outside the central processing of information. We consider this aspect very remarkable.

EXEMPLIFIED PRACTICAL CASE

"Hi, Fred, are you fine? We can begin if you like[1], can't we?" The first item consists of the successive appearance on screen of the letters of TOMATO. Next, he is presented with the screen full of letters in a mess, and we ask him to make the word he saw previously. He answers incorrectly, making the word "POMATO". I say: "I would like[1] to know how[2] you did it." He answers: "by recalling the successive appearance of the letters." I say: what do you mean[3]?" Surprised and disgusted[4], he looks at me and says the same answer. Then, I say: "so what was your head doing as the letters were showing up[5]?" He tells us that he was doing subvocal rehearsal[6]. I say: "well, let's see the sequence of letters again[7]." He bodily frustrated[4]

---

[1] Hypothetical formulation involving an option or experimentation of making decision on the part of the child.

[2] The first crucial question to get the child to make conscious the strategy being used.

[3] Semantic question oriented to get the child to understand the strategy as deeply as possible.

[4] Body language informs us of both cognitive processing and feeling.

[5] This question is complementary of semantic question.

[6] This answer tells us he is using successive processing.

[7] He experiences he is wrong, that is, his mental operation does not work to resolve this problem.

realizes[7] he answered POMATO instead of TOMATO. He looks at me confused[8]. I smile[9] and I add: "so why do you think it happened[10]?" He answers: "I do not know". I continue: "I believe the letters were appearing and we[11] intended to recall it by doing subvocal rehearsal until we have found the meaning; then we[11] have stopped subvocal rehearsal. Later on, when we[11] wrote it on the screen, we[11] remembered the meaning, but not the sequence of letters. Don't you think so?" He answers with a nod, saying yes. I go on: "How or what can we do to prevent it[12]?" He answers he does not know. I say: "You know, maybe[13], we can find some trick." He shakes his head saying no. Then, I suggest[14] that we could imagine[15] a tomato with the word tomato underneath. As I am explaining, I display a tomato on the screen with the word tomato underneath[16].

GOLDEN RULES

On diagnosing and treating, some golden rules must be taken into account. 1. A child should be rewarded for *trying,* not for coming up with the right answer. 2. Initially, lead the child around to the right answer by easy questions. Even if you have to provide the answer, make it look as though he/she really knew the answer but couldn't think of it! 3. For starting a session, always begin by doing material so absurdly simple that your child couldn't possibly fail, allowing the child a few initial triumphs. 4. For stopping a session, always stop a session while your child wants to continue a little longer. 5. For speed of session, "hurry ahead slowly" if possible. For remediation, too fast a pace slows learning!

THE EMOTIONAL APPROACH

The starting point for the ideas to be presented here is that we define as disturbed emotional behavior the showing of what we call masked behavior. That is, a behavior which is masked in the sense what is happening is opaque to the person's own conscious, and even to the others around. These uncontrolled and unconscious behaviors can be considered protective-defensive. Disclosing these behaviors is an important part of the diagnostic and

---

[8] Again, body language tells us both cognitive processing and feeling.

[9] Body language response of educator intending rapport and empathy [Roger, 1959, 1987]. At this point, the aim is not verbal language explanation on the mistake, but empathic feeling communication. The cognitive message in the sense of what is correct and what incorrect is taking place by means of personal experience, that is, the experience of the facts. From the particular experience to generalization according to inductive learning principle.

[10] This question insists on the aim of getting the child to deeply understand the strategy being used inefficiently.

[11] Use of "we" instead of "you". This language formulation prevent the implicit "you have to" and bad feeling associated to the use of "you".

[12] The second crucial question in planning training, which is oriented to get the child to discover a new more efficient strategy to solve the problem.

[13] Again, hypothetical formulation.

[14] The third step oriented to get the child to change the inefficient previously used strategy for a new more efficient strategy, when the child can't find it by himself.

[15] A more efficient simultaneous-based strategy is offered to substitute a more inefficient successive-based one.

[16] Concrete experience must be utilized beyond verbal explanation.

treatment procedure because communicating without fighting against protective behavior is the same as empathy and rapport [Roger 1957, 1989].

Without delay, we must make sure that a diagnostic scheme is always present when we are in front of a masked behavior [Balmes, 1968; Goleman, 1986; Perez-Alvarez & Timoneda-Gallart 1998;Shand, 2000; Mayoral-Rodríguez, 2002; Alabau-Bofill, 2003]. Usually, three markers can be identified: 1. Contradiction between verbal and uncontrolled body language. 2. Contradiction in verbal language arguments. 3. Overreacting-exaggerating-disproportional (cause-effect) behavior. In particular, between the apparent cause of the behavior and the bodily and paravervally bad feeling shown. A fourth marker is generally also present: failure in planning-decision-making.

In the "cognition and emotion" chapter we had already illustrated some instances to see how the above-mentioned markers can be identified. Someone tells us: "Well, I am nervous and I get nervous easily. But children, traffic jams, my secretary, my boss. You know! " We have the clues to diagnose a masked behavior if we find the markers. First, if we get more precise information on the alleged causal factors, then, perhaps, we will conclude we are in the presence of disproportional behavior (first marker). Perhaps, these precipitant factors happened in such a way as not to justify the intensity of the nervous behavior. Second, our patient may not be accompanying his verbal irritation with a congruent body suffering, which is characteristic of the second marker (contradiction between body and verbal language). Perhaps, another person comes in, looks at him/her, and says: "How are you doing?" He/she carelessly answers: "Oh, fine!" Third, our patient two days before did not behave similarly, although the same argued causal factors concurred, which is typical of the third marker (verbal contradiction in arguments). Probably, this person usually will fail in planning-decision-making, although different kinds of masked behavior are possible.

In the previous example, the neocortex of our patient is consciously processing some beliefs, namely, "behaving nervously is an innate characteristic of some persons", " the traffic jam is reason for nervousness", "an incompetent secretary is reason for nervousness", and so on. This belief processing is part of the neo-cortical processing happening in response to the signal coming from the amygdala, which, remember (don't forget), is "a posteriori" produced by using the external information entering via sensorial gates.

At this point, the key question is to define this situation as physiological or, instead, 'pathological'. In other words, the behavioral pattern and, first of all, the painful feeling or discomfort he/she is perceiving must be considered physiological or pathological. We count on another additional marker, the number of painful behaviors the person is putting in action in everyday life. The more painful behaviors, the more pathological the situation is. If the painful feeling is pathological, then the painful feeling is in great part a consequence of the past-memorized painful feeling, but not of the masked present-current event argued.

In neurological terms, what is happening is that the painful feeling processing is operating. As the amygdala is sending signals to all the body, the neocortex also receives this non-cognitive non-informative non-data-content signal and is requested to work. The neocortex gets to work and processes the information entering in real time via sensorial gates and finds a cause-effect relationship between what is externally happening, that is, the nervous behavior and the events that can reasonably justify it. In fact, what the neocortex is doing is simply to operate doing what it is able to do, that is, to reason about, using the memorized knowledge base to find some knowledge (beliefs) that can explain what is happening.

Someone may tell us: "I hit him, he insulted me". If we inquire about the nature of the insult, we'll see how disproportional the response was. Again, the second and third marker we have referred to above will probably be present in this case. Another instance, we put there, would be that a surgeon who devotes more dedication than expected to his/her patient according to the nature of the operation. The disproportional dedication is well apparent at first sight. We said there that someone can argue a "voluntary" over-dedication is laudable and worthy. Of course, this is true, but the matter is the difference between a pleasant over-dedication and an unpleasant one. And we added not only pleasant but also non-compensating pleasant over-dedication.

Now, remember that a good logical reasoning leaves us with the concept of good logical planning linked, in turn, to good decision-making (act of will). In essence, any behavioral change necessarily involves an act of will that implies decision-making. Once again, we must emphasize that any act of will is biologically a behavior and, therefore, must be analyzed as any other behavior.

Therefore, masked decision-making may be formulated as follows: someone definitely tells us: "I want (decision-making) to do that (conscious behavior), for this or that (causal-effect reasons being argued)". We can note incoherent non-reasonable causal-effect relationship (contradiction in verbal arguments and probably overreacting decision according to the reasons argued). Also, he/she tells us with anger (unconsciously triggered body language expressing bad feeling), although he/she verbally affirms he/she is very pleased to make that decision (contradiction verbal-body language) instead of relaxing expression. If what is unconsciously happening is "I am not able / I feel unconfidently badly and I have to behave as I am behaving to feel better releasing tension because this way I am going to feel able", then the decision-making and the act of will are not really a free unconditioned one, leading to a reasonable result or consequence pleasantly felt or, at least, not badly felt. If so, the decision-making act will be "pathologically" painful and, subsequently, the consequences will be also "pathologically" painful, even though the conscious sensation can misleadingly (conscious compensating feeling) be otherwise. Remember (don't forget) the key question is the difference between a non-conditioned decision and a conditioned decision. This last one implies suffering, if only at the unconscious level, and failure in planning.

It is the case of someone who usually behaves with impressive determination and who can be "diagnosed" as an impressive confident personal identity. If this determination is badly experienced-felt, although subconsciously, then the impressive determination is at the expense of impressive effort badly felt. If so, this is a vulnerable situation to cope with any additional stressing factor. So identity, in neurological sensitive terms, can be defined as the set of memorized past painful-emotional experiences linked to their appropriate cognitive-learned beliefs from zero age to current age. By the way, personal beliefs work basically at the central subconscious level beyond what we externally can see, hear, etc. between input of information (event or events as precipitant factors) and output of information (behavioral response) [Das, 1999; Das et al. 1994, 1996, 2000; Timoneda, & Perez-Alvarez, 1996; Perez-Alvarez, 2004].

We can extend our comment on the previous example. He/she is a very confident person behaving with very impressive determination, which is the behavioral pattern he/she is aware of. He/she also tells us he/she is very proud of him/herself, which is the conscious feeling corresponding to the impressive conscious behavior. This pleasant feeling may be either compensating or non-compensating. We'll see next. When he/she tells us it, perhaps, a body expression of "anger" appears, which is the body language communicating painful-unconfident feeling. This does not correspond to relaxing happiness state as it would be expected in good feeling processing. Instead, this behavior may be the compensating behavior in response to a personal belief that we can formulate as " I am not able, I feel badly, therefore I have to behave according to confidence pattern to feel better, although insufficiently to feel quite well." In this point, it is useful to reiterate that the difference between a physiological painful feeling processing and a pathological one is the magnitude or degree. A pathological situation is associated with a practically constant either consciously or more frequently unconsciously unconfident painful living. A better (more physiologically homeostatic) feeling state is possible. The second marker would be unpleasant body expression in contradiction with happy words. Even the third marker could be present in the sense that the reasons alleged to his over-dedication could sometimes be incongruent.

Again, we must remember that the mental mechanism we apply to masked emotional dysfunctional behavior is also applicable to "masked" learning behavior. This last one is what one observes when, working with a particular child, a verbalized strategy is not what is really happening in the act carried out. We interpret that strategy has been unconsciously processed, behavior itself, instead, being processed consciously as it is put into action. In this case, the strategy may be accurately conveyed by body language, for instance, eye movements, whereas linguistic language is saying otherwise.

A behavior put into action to compensate for an unconscious badly unconfident feeling is first felt as a pleasant compensation. In other words, if I'm feeling unconfident, I have to behave to make myself feel better (compensating behavior like, for instance, over-dedication). We also explained there that the feeling sensitivity can be processed both consciously, "I'm feeling badly", and unconsciously, "I'm not aware of any feeling, but I need (I must / I have to) to do uncontrolled behaviors, for instance, over-dedication or not paying attention".

For instance, in the case of a masked compensating aggressive behavior put into action to compensate for the personal badly-unconfident, the person doing the aggressive behavior consciously feels satisfaction, although incomplete satisfaction because an unconscious discomfort is also present. When the compensating behavior becomes insufficient, then the behavior is consciously felt badly, it is felt painfully. And most important, in psychotherapy terms, some cases need to get to this last described stage to be successfully helped.

We remarked there and must insist here on the concept of conscious pleasant compensating feeling associated with behavior compensating for unconscious painful-emotional feeling, in turn, linked to lack of self-confidence, which is neurologically equivalent to a danger signal. We must add that the pleasure of a pleasant compensating behavior is not that of a non-compensating behavior. This last one is like tranquility, relaxation, and peace we can see in body language. As we have said, the personal unconfident feeling can be to a certain extent compensated for by means of compensating masked behaviors, but just to a certain extent; beyond that, the conscious pleasant compensating behavior becomes conscious painful behavior. The body language conveys suffering in both cases, although more obvious in the second.

We had also explained that sometimes the painful feeling, neurologically codified as danger, is consciously experienced, but sometimes it is unconsciously-subconsciously experienced, although painful sensation is a linguistic term linked to consciousness. For instance, the person behaving agressively is not simultaneously aware of his/her conscious bad feeling (we call it rage), but he/she is unconsciously feeling badly and, in fact, the aggressive behavior should be considered a compensating reactive behavior to the bad feeling being unconsciously processed, which allows him/her to feel better, doing the behavior than not doing it. In this condition, the cognitive neocortex of this person is aware of the verbal or/and gesture aggressive behavior unconsciously triggered, but not of the real reason (unconfident-painful feeling) responsible for it.

Let us return to the nervous person above. He/she expresses his bad tempered attitude showing incitement, anger, and rage. This person is aware of the behavioral pattern he/she is doing. This pattern consists of the observable characteristics applicable to the nervous behavior according to the usual linguistic terms. He/she is not aware that he/she is suffering while the behavior happens (unconscious compensating behavior), but could be suffering (conscious insufficient compensating behavior). The nervous behavior is rationally and consciously explained according to learnt and memorized beliefs, in particular, "the traffic jam is reason for nervousness", "an incompetent secretary is reason for nervousness", and so on. Remember the what-are-you-doing and the six-month-old-baby metaphor, where we explained how explanations are "fabricated" as an "a posteriori" thought.. Remember also the beliefs can be linguistically formulated as "A is/has B". Apparently, all seems reasonable, but a good reasoning may be absent, and if so, then the nervous behavior is a perfect masked behavior for oneself and the others, and the real reason for the nervous behavior is the unconfident-painful sensitivity component of the memorized unconscious personal beliefs, which can be both cognitively and sensitively formulated as " I am not able / I am feeling badly and unconfident". We note the importance of body language to get to know the person is suffering. In our illustrative case, he/she is surely suffering because the uncontrolled and unconsciously triggered body language tells us it: "He/she expresses his bad tempered attitude showing incitement and anger."

Like the cognitive approach, the emotional approach also implies the diagnosis of beliefs. To diagnose beliefs is like the old Zen saying: if you give a man a fish, you feed him for a day, but if you teach him to fish, you feed him for a lifetime. We can illustrate the procedure according to the following scheme:

DIAGNOSIS				INTERVENTION
Behavior **He/she says** + **He/she does**	Belief **A** *is / is not* B	Personal Belief **Identity** *I can't... / I feel incapable* *I feel insecure* *I feel badly* *I feel guilty*	Pain	
1	2	3	4	

1. "Look, I'm very nervous. You know, my children are so naughty. Furthermore, the traffic jam is unbearable. I can't stand it any longer! On the other hand, my secretary is getting worse and worse, and my boss is becoming a lunatic". - He talks with strong words and provocative gestures; his face reflects anger.

2. Being nervous is constitutional / Naughty children provoke a nervous state. / traffic jams causes nervous state / And so on.

3. *I can't / I feel insecure / I feel badly / I feel guilty* if I'm not nervous and a series of factors or situations cause my nervous behavior. Whenever one processes *"I feel badly"* associated with a behavior, simultaneously one processes *cause-effect relationship badly.* We call this feeling badly *blame*

sentiment. This sentiment may be either unconsciously or consciously processed, depending on the efficacy of the compensating behavior.

4. Body and paraverbal language expressing unpleasant sensation.

DIAGNOSIS	INTERVENTION			
	Behavior I say + I do	Belief A *is / is not* B	Personal Belief Identity *I can.../ I'm capable* *I feel secure* *I feel well* *Versus* *I can't / I feel incapable* *I feel insecure* *I feel badly*	Pain
	1	2	3	4

1. Look, it is amazing! I remember what happened to me years ago. Someone phoned me and asked me: "I would like to invite you to a conference on ... We have thought you could talk about .... ", in fact, a theme I was very familiar with. Do you know what happened? I looked at my agenda with concern. If my agenda was full, I relaxed and I apologized to him/her. However, do you know what happened otherwise? I didn't agree immediately. In fact, I tried finding some excuse, I believed it, to apologize and avoid the situation. Really, do you know why? I felt insecure, I was suffering just thinking I was going to assume that compromise. Next, I change the discourse to produce amnesia post-trance.

2. What we do is not always what we are / What we see as a cause is not always the real cause of the behavior

3. *I can / I feel secure, confident / I feel well versus I can't / I feel badly /I feel insecure/ I feel guilty.*

4. Pacing.

As we can see, both diagnosis and remediation meet the scheme we have just illustrated above. Remember (don't forget) the beliefs like the strategies in the cognitive approach meet the principle according to which both of them are central processing, but not either input or output. We can exemplify: someone tells me "idiot" (input triggering-precipitant causal factor), which is equivalent to "tell me how ' b u s' is pronounced" (input of information). The answer in response to "idiot" is a verbal and non-verbal aggressive behavior (output). What matters is the central mental processing, supporting the personal identity, in terms of beliefs that can be formulated as follows: "idiot is worthless and painful; I'm unable and worthless and I feel badly if/because I feel idiot". Really, the neurons at the amygdala are supposed to be codifying danger in a situation like this one. This way, both cognitive processing and emotional processing work interactively. Obviously, the magnitude of the behavioral response will be different depending on the personal belief (identity). The more convinced that I'm an idiot, the more overreacting-exaggerating-disproportional behavioral response (masked behavior).

This scheme is always operating in such a way that you can substitute the causal factor "you are an idiot" for any other factor, for instance, "you are not intelligent" or simply, "a bad experience at school", or "a bad experience at home". Most important, verbal language is not necessary at all. The data informative content can be classified into linguistic data (propositional data) via visual or auditory channels and non-linguistic data (analogic data) as it is "somebody laughing or shouting or judging" via visual, auditory or tactile channels. At central processing, propositional data (thought, language) or/and analogic data (images, sounds, smells, tastes) are equally processed from the point of view of beliefs.

The personal belief with its both cognitive and feeling component is mentally constructed and memorized according to the processing we are going to elaborate on now. A whatever experience with not only a verbal component but also a body component (para-verbal language included) is caught up by the sensorial gates and either consciously or more frequently unconsciously processed at the central level where either consciously or more frequently unconsciously a belief is constructed. We will insist that the external information can be verbal, for instance, "you are stupid", but also non-verbal, for instance, "a bad experience at school" or "a bad experience at home". The fact is that positively experienced input leads to " I'm able // I feel well // confident", but instead negative experienced input leads to "I'm not able // I feel badly // unconfident". If this last option is the case, then "I must / I have to / I need to" (see later chest....metaphor) put into action compensating behaviors to make myself feel better (compensation). This process happens unconsciously until compensating behaviors are insufficient. Then conscious painful feeling processing takes place.

Remember once again that the belief can be formulated as A is/has-have B as we have just explained. Immediately, after a belief has been constructed (internalized and memorized), a personal belief is also extrapolated by means of a implicit-unconscious process generally. The personal belief can be linguistically formulated as "I am (able) or I am not (able) if ..." [cognitive component to be memorized by cognitive neurons] and "I feel well or badly if ..." [feeling-sensitive component to be memorized by the sensitive neurons]. The "if ..." corresponds to the extrapolated belief from which the personal belief is built up. In the case of masked behavior the previous formulation can be masked as follows: "I am 'able' / I feel 'well' // 'confident' if I behave doing the masked behavior".

It must be added that the "well / bad" feeling is equivalent to either conscious or unconscious "confident / unconfident", because feeling-sensitive neurons really codify danger. So, for instance, a belief considered valuable (value) by everybody is "being intelligent is capability, it is being worthy". Then, "I am able / worthy // I feel well / confident if I am intelligent". The opposite "I'm not able / worthy // I feel badly / unconfident" if I am not intelligent. The cognitive component is memorized by the cognitive neurons, and the associated feeling is memorized by the feeling neurons.

According to the evidence we are discussing through the discussion, we postulate that our brain memorize not only a 'knowledge base' but also a 'feeling base'. So, two kinds of painful feeling processing can be differentiated, one happening when the memorized personal painful beliefs ('feeling base' linked to personal identity in psycholinguistic terms) are being processed, and the other happening when the current-present painful event (precipitant causal factor) is being processed. Both of them have to do with the exogenous experiences lived by the person and the particular endogenous characteristic of the person in question. The fact is that every person has a 'sensitive brain', not codifying informative data that works as an alarm system to protect us. The triggering threshold can be such that the 'cognitive brain' works under the order of the 'sensitive brain'.

There are a number of key practical points that we wish to illustrate next.

We will summarize the most usual indirect communication techniques [Grinder et al. 1978; Erickson & Rossi, 1981; Watzlawick, 1985] in the following box:

Indirect Communication Techniques

```
INDIRECT COMMUNICATION TECHNIQUES

* Anchor / analogic underlining
* Anticipation
* Channels overloading
* Concrete processing
* Confusion
* Describing instead of judging
* ERICKSONIAN HYPNOSIS
* False alternative option
* Linguistic formulation:
* Ask-for-help formulation
     * Ambiguous terms
     * Dissociation
     * Hypothetical terms
     * "I / we" instead of "you" formulation
     * Masked reference (masked negation)
     * METAPHOR
     * Phrases,clauses, and sentences:
          * Included words
          * Introductory words
   * Questions:
          * Masked question
          * Open question
          * Semantic question
* Pacing
* Pattern break (interruption of pattern of processing)
* Prompting (making decision favoring or inducing)
* Prescription of symptom
* Silence
* Strategic performing
```

Keeping the above box in mind, we must devote ourselves to help master the diagnosis-intervention of masked behaviors:

MASKED DEFENSIVE BEHAVIOR

"I'm not an authoritarian guy!" He shows an angry look[17]. I accept it[18]. I do not argue[18]. He proceeds: "Yeah, I know children must understand their parents are confident friends.

---

[17] Contradiction between verbal language and body language. His body language communicates discomfort that can be assessed as exaggerating reaction to causal factors being argued next.

[18] Verbal and body pacing. We are in front of a masked behavior due to badly feeling processing, but not to rational-reflexive thinking. The purpose of this behavior is releasing tension, but not explaining anything. The therapeutic dialogue for a tension state is both saying and doing (body language), not increasing bad feeling. In fact, the better dialogue for a feeling state is not linguistic language, but body language. The expression "I accept" means I don't say anything against, but above all I do in such way that I don't bodily convey a painful

Everyday, I say Gerard he may do what he wishes, but, do you know, there are rules that must be met: coming home on time, making the bed, studying, explaining to us what he does, where he goes, and so on[19]. I want him to make decisions[19] in the future." As he talks, he bangs on the table[20] and adds: "You know, am I behaving authoritarian? I accept both verbally and bodily[21]. Silence[22]... He changes the focus of attention[23], and starts talking about his son's friends, saying that he does not like them at all.

A deep-seated masked behavior becomes a masked resistance behavior:

MASKED RESISTANCE BEHAVIOR

She comes with her mother. She looks angry[24]. I ask her if she wants to come in[25]. She, annoyed says no with a nod[26]. As I stood in silence[27], her mother tries to convince her. She comes in and I ask her if she does not mind[28] her mother waits outside. Again, she says no with a nod[26]. There is no eye contact[29] with me; she looks around. I do not comment[30]. I begin

---

provoking message. To be successful, it is necessary my personal identity (personal beliefs) as a therapist is not hurt by the behavior. If hurt, I won't be able to avoid communicating my pain, at least, bodily.

[19] Contradiction in verbal arguments. Although he argues his son is allowed to make decisions, what we can deduce of his argumentation is a considerable unquestioned control over him.

[20] Again, contradiction between verbal and body language. New exaggerating reaction to causal factors being argued.

[21] Verbal and body pacing.

[22] Application of silence associated with pacing body language. Here is applicable what is exposed in point two. Silence must be applied being aware of not provoking discomfort in the person I am speaking to. We call this silence a productive silence in the sense that our silence is always followed by a resuming initiative of the other. Regarding verbal production, generally, a change of focus of conversation takes place in response to silence application. This is reasonable because the ongoing discourse is a masked verbal behavior due to badly feeling processing. In fact, the discourse is an "a posteriori" production.

[23] Change of focus of conversation in response to pacing. Characteristically, the early discourse is a reactive fighting attitude against his son due to the internal personal discomfort. Pacing prevents this attitude from being reinforced. Instead, pacing decreases the personal internal discomfort, raises the triggering sensitivity threshold, and subsequently the conversation focus is translated from against-his-son to himself, that is, from outside to inside. This process is always indicative of an efficient empathy or rapport {Roger 1957, 1989].

[24] Body language that denotes painful feeling processing (discomfort). As always (don't forget), body language informs us about feeling processing, regardless the linguistic language.

[25] Prompting. It is about a procedure to induce decision-making. Since the beginning, this is the basic goal the educator pursues. The most important inductive learning is to make the individual experience many different decision-making contexts in order for him/her to internalize and transfer the principle "I can / I am confident". The basic therapeutic aim is to provide counterweight in the sense that the more confident feeling memorizes, the less fearful-painful unconfident feeling memorizes. Remember that the reward and the punishment are neurologically memorized according to an inversely proportional principle. Don't forget that both a lack of decision-making experience and an excessive moral criticizing attitude are the most negatively powerful factors contributing to an unconfident identity.

[26] Body language communicating feeling. We will see later whether it is about an overreacting behavior taking into account the reasons of her anger.

[27] Here is applicable what is explained in point six about masked behavior.

[28] Prompting technique. See point two above.

[29] Body language in way of eye contact. This attitude reflects a "flight" behavior, the opposite of "fight" behavior. Both behaviors are typical masked defensive-protective behaviors indicating badly-unconfident feeling processing.

[30] Verbal pacing as an adequate response to feeling processing. Don't forget that verbal pacing must always be accompanied by congruent body language. To master this congruency capacity, a personal identity coherent

my discourse. I introduce myself[31]. Next, I explain to her who I am and what I do[30]. She remains in silence, looks down[32]. I accept and I do not comment[33] I follow by telling her that I will not do anything without her approval[34]. Then, she gives me an angry look[35] and says with an angry tone[35] of voice: "I have no problem at all"[36]. I do not argue[37]. Silence[37]... She follows: "I am an excellent student and I have no problem[35] at home, and I and my friends get along splendidly." Again, I do not argue[36]. I accept her arguments both verbally and bodily[36]. Next, she says once again. "I have no problem[35] at all".

We will center now on the following practical resort:

DIRECTED ERICKSONIAN HYPNOSIS

We need the right time and place. Our patient must maintain the right position, comfortable with eyes closed to avoid distracting visual stimuli. We must talk with the appropriate slow rhythm and monotonous para-verbal language inviting to tranquility and avoiding distracting acoustic stimuli. Next, we must saturate all the channels (inputs) of information in order working memory to overwork, such that attention must be extremely concentrated on a limited quantity of information. This way, during hypnosis [Grinder et al. 1978; Erickson & Rossi, 1981; Watzlawick, 1985], the information cognitively processed and the associated feeling processed will be that which we will favor. As a result, a good comfortable-relaxing feeling processing will take place associated (anchored to) with a cognitive content. Although, traditionally, the cognitive-informative content, which is given as a suggestion, has been considered substantial in the procedure, we are convinced that hypnosis works out because of relaxing effect rather than because of any other sophisticated effect. The message conveyed as a final suggestion becomes a verbal resort (verbal anchor) to favor recalling of the experience.

We can teach them a relaxation exercise. We can teach them how to breath properly and deeply by directing their breath to the lowest part of their abdomen first and then to fill up his

---

with the framework we are explaining through the book is needed. These idees must be part of our beliefs or convictions. Otherwise, our uncontrolled body language will reflect our subconsciously felt beliefs.

[31] Anticipation and subtle application of prompting. Anticipation because in so far as I introduce myself, my patient can foresee what is coming, which releases tension and fear. Any painful-fearful factor plays against our purpose. However, not only this effect is produced, but also we are subtly making our patient experience autonomy in the sense his/her brain processes he/she individually copes with a particular situation.

[32] See point six.

[33] Verbal and body pacing.

[34] Prompting and anticipation.

[35] Verbal and body expressions of resistance. She bodily conveys subconscious painful feeling. Although we are intending to make her feel better enough as to diminish her masked behavior, we fail in tearing down the defense.

[36] Contradiction between verbal and body language. "I have no problem, but I am unconsciously feeling badly". Maybe, we can assure that we are in the presence of overreacting-exaggerating-disproportional behavior. I mean that the magnitude of her behavior in response to my intervention is not reasonable. Resistance appears again and again.

[37] In front of the defense we must apply pacing technique not to reinforce it. Remember we are receiving feeling in way of this behavior, but not really rational and logical-based arguments. Contra-arguments do not make sense. Strictly speaking, we are deeply involved in a feeling "dialogue", but not in a linguistic dialogue. At first sight, it may look absurd, but things are not always what they appear to be.

chest. A full breath starts by filling up the abdomen, then the chest. Just as the chest becomes completely full, the clavicle, or collarbone, will rise slightly, which we can observe. Then both cavities will empty. The breath should be slow and smooth, without stop or interruptions. This is followed by a relief sensation. Next, we tell them to shake out the tension in their neck and shoulders by wiggling their hands and arms and rolling their heads around in slow circles. The following are common body cues (muscular indicators) indicating discomfort: raised or tight shoulders, slumped shoulders, arms or/and shoulders held back, slumped appearance, chest caved in, stiff or tight jaw, wrinkled or strained forehead, and so on.

Hypnotic communication is practically always rounded off by amnesia post-trance. This phenomenon can be exemplified as follows: a little child is shown 8 pencils and told "Take 5 for your teacher, just count out 5." He/she simply counts the 8 pencils. Child is so focussed (attention) on the counting process than they forget (amnesia) the target, that is, he/she doesn't hold the goal in working memory. Or, likewise, he/she counts:" 1,2,3, oh, oh, yeah! 5." He/she has to stop and think what comes after 3 when counting a set of 5 items. He/she has to focus a great deal of attention (working memory) on keeping track and not misproduce the number sequence, skipping a number. He/she suffered from amnesia.

A SIMPLE RESORT TO DIAGNOSE
UNCONSCIOUS TENSION (INSECURITY)

It is convenient for the patient to be lying down. I speak to him/her in a slow, relaxed, pleasant, and care-free voice. And the tone of my voice is lower and "softer" in feeling as well as volume. I intend the calm tone of my voice to become an anchor for him/her. Talking very slowly and carefully, I match the pace of my voice with the rise and fall of his/her chest as he/she breathed in and out. I start as follows: I would like[38] to do a play consisting of you going, with your mind's eye, to some place, for instance, the beach, cinema, or another place you like[38]. You may[38] be walking along a beach, walking through the woods, sitting down in a large field of flowers, and so forth. You may choose any of those settings. Your eyes should be closed and I'll ask you some questions you may answer as you like[38]. Well, I need you tell me where you'll go, OK[39]? I start questioning intending to saturate channels of information[40].

---

[38] Hypothetical terms application. In fact, this formulation makes its effect by means of the implicit prompting effect. This formulation is neurologically and psycholinguistically processed as an experience of choosing or opting-out, that is, decision making in the sense oneself decides the comment is applicable to oneself. What is clear and widely accepted is that the hypothetical formulation makes, the person we are speaking to, feel better than when we use more direct linguistic communication.

[39] Prompting application. The more unconfident personality (identity), the less determination we observe. A resort like this may provide us with a striking clues about insecurity. We can see the extraordinary difficulty some persons, not only children, have to decide so much irrelevant point. But don't be wrong, we are convinced from our experience that we can reach a successful therapeutic effect by favoring or inducing our patient to experience decision making acts so simple as this one. It is not about making transcendental decisions. No, absolutely not! The practice of decision making act makes our brain memorize security. And do not forget. The purpose of this therapy is to provide pleasant-confident feeling-sensitivity to our brain to counterweight the painful-fearful unconfident sensitivity early memorized.

[40] Channels saturation technique. This is an excellent resort to practice ericksonian hypnosis [Grinder et al. 1978; Erickson & Rossi, 1981; Watzlawick, 1985]. Remember that Ericksonian hypnosis works by producing extremely focussing of attention. The saturation of channels of information causes confusion, which means a

My questions[41] have to do with what he/she sees (persons, things), hears (movements, voices) touches (persons, things), smells (of the air), feels (temperature), and so forth[42]. Next, we'll ask as many questions as to get him to visualize what is around him in way of colors, forms, places, weather, persons and so on. Other questions will go oriented to experience sounds, smells, feelings. It is about hearing language beyond the meaning of the words. I don't let him/her take many times to answer.[43] As I am questioning, I am looking for body clues[44] of tension. Simultaneously, I am touching[45] his/her ankles, and alternatively raise the right or the left leg. This maneuver reliably tells us the muscular tone, which is directly related to the tension state. While doing this, I continue to look for body clues. This is a simple technique that allows us to identify unconscious feeling-tension state. The more tension, the less collaboration.

Case 1

A 15 year-old-girl is being treated because of anorexia. During an interview with her, she says she is fat. At this moment, I ask her what she means[46] by "fat". She answers: "I have a large belly". Then, I ask her with a slow, relaxed, pleasant, and care-free voice[47]: "Well, if

---

limitation in the scope (span) of the attention. Achieving this aim, we make the cerebral processing and its supporting neurons in activity be those dedicated to cognitively process and sensitively feel what I communicate both cognitively and sensitively (feeling). We communicate above all pleasant feeling. This means we manage to put out of service the rest of the consciously operating brain, mainly, the painful-fearful processing brain responsible for the masked cognitive processing (illogical rationalization) and resistance behavior. This way Ericksonian hypnosis works on the base of a neurological rationale beyond any esoteric speculation. We will explain in other moment how the resort we call anchor (anchoring) is practically always present in the ericksonian hypnosis.

[41] Question formulation is a communicative technique that involves ericksonian hypnosis as far as, in front of a question, it makes the brain be obliged to think and, simultaneously, to pay attention, to concentrate on the matter. Furthermore, question formulation implicitly implies the prompting application. Any answer to any question involves an option, that is, more than one possible answer. This is a decision making act.

[42] Channels saturation and concrete processing. We can see the realization of the channels saturation resorting to having the individual put in service all the sensorial inputs of information processing. Putting aside this, we can also see here how Ericksonian hypnosis pursues learning internalization and far transferring of what is being processed by using concrete knowledge instead of abstract message. Concrete knowledge (objects, tangible informative data) makes easier paying attention, memorization, internalization and transference. On the other hand, feeling processing is more linked to concrete than abstract processing. Like Picasso painting, abstraction creation comes from concrete reality.

[43] Pattern break technique. It consists of doing something to break the processing of information on course. This contributes to confusion, that is, difficulty paying attention, which makes it necessary to concentrate on more and more. So Ericksonian hypnosis keeps on.

[44] Body language is always the informative feed back.

[45] Again, pattern break of information processing.

[46] Semantic question application. This question allows us to verify how the literal linguistic formulation does not agree with its conceptual meaning. This is typical of masked verbal language, which is a consequence of feeling, but not of reflexive thinking. On the other hand, any question produces an Ericksonian hypnosis effect.

[47] Para-verbal language application oriented to convey a feeling of well being. We must remember that an anchorage effect is continuously occurring during the procedure. The most relevant anchorage effect is between the feeling of the person we are assisting and the experience being lived, and subsequently between feeling and the therapist (empathy - rapport).

you like[48], close your eyes[49] and try and see into your belly". I continue to ask how she sees her belly[50]. Next questions[51] have to do with what he/she sees (persons, things), hears (movements, voices) touches (persons, things), smells (of the air), feels (temperature), and so on[52]. We try do to get him to visualize what is around it in way of colors, forms, and so forth. Other questions will go oriented to experience sounds, smells, feelings. Then, she goes on: "I am feeling a weight, a burden"[53]. I say: "Could[54] you tell me something more?" She adds: "It is a huge burden!". When the description is over, I add that her brain can blast the weight and release her belly[55]. Once her body language[56] translates pleasant relief, I shift my focus of conversation to another unrelated point[57]. For instance, I ask her about the film she viewed last week. Minutes later, she suddenly says: "Look, I am fine[58]!"

---

[48] Hypothetical term. Remember that this linguistic formulation makes its effect by means of the implicit prompting effect. It is about an experience of choosing or opting-out, and therefore a decision-making experience. What is evident is that the hypothetical formulation makes the person we are speaking to feel better than when we use more direct linguistic communication.

[49] As far as a channel of information is closed, the concentration is more easily reached. Furthermore, the compliance or non-compliance is an excellent marker of feelings state. The more tension, the less compliance. It goes without saying that non-compliance shows resistance and to go with it is not indicated.

[50] Again, semantic question.

[51] Question application continues with the subsequent Ericksonian hypnosis effect. Remember that questions imply Ericksonian hypnosis effect. In front of a question, the brain is obliged to think and, simultaneously, to pay attention, to concentrate on the matter. Then, other different matters, among them what is producing painful unconfident feeling, are put aside. Furthermore, question formulation implicitly implies the prompting application. Any answer to any question involves an option, that is, more than one possible answer. This is a decision-making act.

[52] Concrete processing induction. This doing is crucial in any hypnotic process. The brain under hypnotic condition and therefore under limited span of attention needs to operate the most concrete knowledge to keep the concentration state on and on. The more abstract knowledge is required, the more neuronal areas are also required and therefore the less concentration is reached. Remember we postulate that the hypnotic effect is basically due to analgesic effect (relaxing effect). Relaxing effect by itself produces not only short term but also long term therapeutic effect. This relaxing effect happens because during hypnotic state it is felt the cognitive content being processed, but not other different cognitive content. That's why, it is reasonable to deduce, masked verbal rationalization as a reactive response to painful feeling is put aside. This, in turn, involves that the person under this state is in a better condition to receive any cognitive content that won't be fought and refused. Any content that is fought and refused is likewise not well memorized.

[53] The person we are speaking to processes concrete knowledge and expresses her feeling in the form of tangible knowledge.

[54] Again, hypothetical term formulation.

[55] This formulation corresponds to a suggestion in hypnotic terms. What is pursued here is the patient, under hypnotic state, mentally lives an experience. The effect is produced because a experience is mentally lived, which means a cognitive content is processed by the brain, and simultaneously felt. The feeling effect is a pleasant feeling effect.

[56] As always, the body language is utilized as an efficient feedback to proceed.

[57] Amnesia post-trance application. As we have already said, hypnotic communication is practically always rounded off by amnesia post-trance. The purpose for this technique is to avoid the person leaving hypnotic state to become a masked rationalization producer because of the resumed painful feeling processing. Once the relaxing effect has been obtained, we must do in order to keep on. It makes no sense to start a discussion on this or that. It is not profitable at all.

[58] The technique itself consists of suddenly shifting attention (working memory) to another focus, which breaks pattern of information processing leading to an effort of concentration in front of the confusion coming up. In fact, we are practicing Ericksonian hypnosis. This move causes amnesia for the previous experience.

Case 2

Jaime, a 34-year-old father whom we are interviewing starts crying[59]. I say: "Jaime, I think you are in a painful darkness"[60]. He says yes with a nod[61]. I continue: "Look, if you like[62], close your eyes and see yourself inside[63]". I am talking softly, pacing my voice[64]. He closes his eyes and breathes deeply[65]. I say him: "Please, how / what is this darkness like?"[66]. He tells me: "It is like a bricked-up window, black in color"[67]. I add: "What do you believe there is on the other side of the window?[68]" He says anxiously[69]: "Nothing, nothing, but, maybe, I can't see it". I continue: "If Jaime[70] likes[71], he can knock down the wall[72]". Bodily,

---

[59] Body language behavior of conscious painful feeling. This behavior is also subject to be analyzed as a possible marker of masked behavior. We mean that contradiction between verbal and body language and proportion or disproportion between crying behavior and reasons being argued must be analyzed in order to diagnose masked behavior.

[60] Concrete symbolic processing induction is practiced here without delay because we know from the follow-up of the therapy it is appropriate. In fact, we are inducing directed Ericksonian hypnosis in this way.

[61] Body language feedback. Communication in concrete terms is rapidly established as expected. We are doing it correctly.

[62] Hypothetical term application.

[63] Move to facilitate concentration and therefore Ericksonian hypnosis.

[64] Application of para-verbal language oriented to convey a feeling of well-being and to establish an anchorage effect between the feeling of the person we are assisting and the experience being lived (empathy - rapport).

[65] Body language feedback of compliance and non-resistance.

[66] Concrete symbolic processing induction is reinforced.

[67] Dialogue based on concrete processing keeps on. As you can see, the concrete linguistic terms are used to externally express feeling. In fact, this corresponds to what we know as sentiment externalizing in psychological terms. This phenomenon of externalizing sentiments (feelings) is a good indicator of resistance or non-resistance attitude. The more resistance, the less sentiment externalization. By the way, frequently we hear or read that the person with problems must externalize his/her sentiments to improve his/her state. Then, according to this principle what the therapist must do is to say to the patient exactly this direct verbal message: "You must externalize your feeling to ameliorate and recover". But we know this does not work frequently. Why? Let's do an analysis about etiological mechanism according to our theoretical framework. We interpret that non-externalization of feeling is a masked resistance behavior due to painful unconfident personal feeling, but not a consequence of will. Then, a person will be able to externalize his/her sentiments when his/her personal unconfident painful feeling changes to the better. This change is not affordable via understanding (Bandura, 1969), but feeling, although by means of understanding (knowledge processing) feeling happens. Personal feeling sensitivity being continuously processed at the neurological level is changeable by means of new experiences that are cognitively and sensitively processed, increasing good feeling and decreasing bad feeling. Or, in other words, increasing confidence and decreasing non-confidence. The experience of choosing or opting-out, that is, decision making is basic. Unconditional support, compatible with discipline learning, on the part of the parents is also basic when we are dealing with childhood period.

[68] Conducted dialogue based on concrete symbolic processing keeps on.

[69] Body language feedback informs us of a painful unconfident feeling. It doesn't matter knowing details about what is causing this state. In fact, he probably doesn't know what in particular is producing it. Don't forget our purpose is not a cognitive analysis.

[70] Dissociation technique. In front of a quite painful feeling moment, dissociation is an effective procedure to cope with the situation. Dissociation consists of using the name of our patient instead of "you" when we speak to him/her. This makes him/her feel better. This effect is psycholinguistacally based on the fact that any cognitive content is processed associated with its feeling content. When we speak to someone in terms of "you", the person receiving our communication processes the information such that it is more intensively felt than when dissociation is practiced. In psychological terms, it is said that dissociation makes the brain delude itself in front of the same message that, however, is felt differently.

[71] Again, hypothetical term application.

[72] Suggestion.

he shows fear and doubt[73]. He does not dare to proceed. I go on: "I am going to help you[74]. Look, do you hear the hammer at the wall?" He relaxes. I continue: "We are making holes in the wall. What do you see on the other side[75]?" He smiles and relaxed[76] says: "I can see my home town, my family, my countryside, my friends[77]". He looks relaxed[78] and I resort to amnesia post-trance[79]. "Do you know what time it is?"

We will proceed to make some comments on several useful indirect communication techniques:

ANCHOR / ANCHORING

Anchoring is simply a relationship or association. In PASS terms, then, we are dealing with simultaneous processing. Mood states may be anchored to a particular setting and information like sights, sounds, smells and tastes. Different places and people don't look, sound, smell, do the same by any means. Anchoring is almost unbelievably powerful. We can anchor (associate) any experience to feeling. The possibilities are almost limitless. A visual image like the face of a particular person, sounds, words, touch (hand on shoulder or touching a hand while talking) are all potential successful anchors. Definitely, any experience can be anchored to a pleasant feeling state.

PACING

Pacing is a term introduced by neurolinguistic programming (NLP) [Grider at ...]. We have adopted it to refer to the verbal and body behavior that "paces" the verbal and body language of the individual we are interviewing. Although pacing semantically implies rhythm, the concept involved here is getting closer to our patient.

Anna is 16 years of age and comes to our office because of anorexia. I plan an interview with her mother[80]. Her mother tells me: "My daughter is a liar and obstinate girl. She is

---

[73] Again, body language feedback tells us painful feeling processing is taking place. In fact, this somewhat shows a resistance behavior. He is reluctant to feel better, although this attitude mustn't be considered a will decision after a rational processing. This resistance attitude means that painful unconfident feeling is still enough to produce a reactive refusal to be able to feel better. First it is feeling, then it is will. Will will be able to act once unconfident feeling changes into confident enough. Unconfident feeling will change into confident feeling by means of experiences of decision making and unconditional support.

[74] Unconditional support experience.

[75] With the same purpose, concrete symbolic processing keeps on

[76] Body language feedback has just changed to better in feeling terms. Resistance has just broken down

[77] Concrete symbolic processing is utilized to express feeling state.

[78] Peaceful body language feedback remains.

[79] Amnesia post-trance is applied according to what we have already explained

[80] This is an example of strategic performing. We claim that body language and by extension facts language is more reliably (credibility) processed by the brain than linguistic language. Furthermore, any experienced situation (facts) is much better learnt, felt, and memorized than any knowledge not based on tangible facts. On this base, we decide to interview the mother instead of the daughter. The mother, not the daughter, asks for help for her daughter. Under this fact, the belief of the mother is that the problem is my daughter exclusively. Our diagnosis based on our experience is the problem is not exclusively the daughter. We practice this strategic

always right. She does not accept any criticism. She can not be questioned at all". Disgust, anger, and rage are gradually shown on her face[81]. I do not contra-argue. I accept both verbally and bodily. I say to her: "You must feel so badly! You can not understand why your daughter behaves in this thoughtless and inconsiderate way. I see"[82]. The mother nods her head, looks down, tears comes to her eyes, and shifts her focus of attention-conversation, by saying: "She does not eat either"[83].

SILENCE

The father comes alone. He tells me both he and his son are doing better. His 14-year-old boy had been admitted to a hospital in critical condition because of life-threatening asthmatic disease with a high psycogenic etiological factor. That is the way this case came to our office. At present, he had been discharged from the hospital. The father sits down, smiling and relaxed[84]. I do not say anything. I also sit down. I smile. I silently wait[85]. He starts talking. He explains he is considering doing a trip to his village. He stops. I do not say anything. I look at him with no worry and I wait[86]. He smiles and continues by saying that he has been offered a

---

performance to indirectly communicate what we have just said. We do not directly tell the mother something like: "Look, madam, you are part of the problem". We do not do it. This direct communication conveys painful feeling and, although our patient verbally accepts it, we must affirm that it is not empathic communication. We do not gain anything. This does not contribute to rapport. Absolutely not! Don't forget. The therapeutic success is not a question of understanding, but a question of feeling.

[81] Both verbal linguistic language and body language show painful feeling. This is not a case of contradiction between verbal and body language. However, the verbal reasons being argued to implicitly justify her anger are quite suspicious in the sense that exaggeration can be applied for her verbal behavior. She didn't even mention just a positive value of her daughter. Remember "fighting" behavior as a response to personal painful feeling adopts this disproportional criticizing attitude against the other. The other is the hurting precipitant causal factor, but not the basic causal factor, which has to do with the personal identity of the mother.

[82] Verbal and body pacing in response to painful feeling. To contra-argue doesn't make sense. As you can see, however, this instance of pacing shows a non-short linguistic component. However, you can also see the linguistic component is not a contra-argument centered on what the mother said, but a comment on feeling.

[83] Usually, if resistance masked behavior is not present, we observe this empathic outcome. Pacing rapport produces an increasing feeling effect leading to a non-masked expression of feeling. The mask disappears and the defense breaks down. This event is an excellent indicator of successful therapy. The success is always in feeling, but not in understanding. However, a faint resistance masked behavior fights to remain when she shifts the focus of conversation to talk about the eating problem of her daughter again. The change of focus characteristically happens for leaving a feeling experience as a form of resistance, but also as a way of keeping verbal masked behavior in response to pacing. Someone is explaining what can be typified as verbal masked behavior, the therapist applies pacing, and the person shifts the focus because the conversation is really a masked argument due to painful feeling.

[84] Body language information about state of mind, in particular, feeling state.

[85] Silence implementation. This is an excellent resort when pacing is needed. In this occasion, however, silence basically pursues to reach productive silence, that is, to obtain verbal and body information. As a therapeutic principle, whenever we consider we have nothing to say according to an objective, we must receive information. Our decision to act will be based on diagnosis-intervention of beliefs. Remember that silence application implies pattern break of information processing, which forces attention concentration and therefore makes Ericksonian hypnosis grow. We will break our silence when we observe by means of body language feedback we are producing unnecessary tension.

[86] New implementation of silence. Silence technique of communication requires an appropriate body communication on the part of those who are practicing it. We mean we mustn't convey personal unconscious tension. We must remain relaxed. To be successful, we must be convinced (belief) this resort works and makes sense.

new more lucrative job. I say: "Congratulations! Excellent news!" I match these verbal expressions with coherent body manifestations[87]. He follows: "My son agrees. However, I am a bit doubtful. It involves a change of home. You know. These sort of things". I am aware I am in front of a masked question[88]. He is expecting my opinion to make decision about it. I remain in silence[89]. Next, he spontaneously continues: "Yeah, yes, of course, I believe I need a change. I will accept the offer". I do not comment on anything. Simply, I answer with a nod of agreement[90]. He breaths deeply relaxed and gets up. We shake our hands and he goes out.

FOCUS OF CONVERSATION

No sooner had she arrived than she started talking. I do not contra-argue her. I look at her in silence[91]. Immediately, she proceeds. She talks of her parents to blame[92] them for several things. For instance, she angrily[93] says they did not take her with them to go to dinner on Sundays and, instead, they left her with her grandmother[94]. I accept both verbally and bodily[95]. She bitterly[96] adds that her mother calls her monster, and that they (her parents) are responsible for[92] her failure in school and refusal of her friends[97]. I do not contra-argue. I accept her discourse and her body language[98]. As I look at her, I quietly remain in silence[99].

---

[87] Verbal and body language coherence.

[88] Prompting implementation. "My son agrees. However, I am a bit doubtful. It involves a change of home. You know. These sort of things." The father is formulating a masked question, that is, he is questioning without saying the question in explicit grammatical terms. In fact, he is experiencing the uncertainty under which he is in front of a decision. He is seeking our endorsement.

[89] We practice silence in order to make him make decision. Making decisions we build our personal identity: self-steem and self-confidence. Any decision involves a risk of mistake, but this risk and the experience of mistaken decision must be experienced. Everybody has the right to be wrong. The more mistaken decisions we make, the less confident our identity is. The more mistaken decisions we make, the more help we need. How this help is done is what this therapeutic procedure is bringing up.

[90] When the decision has been made, we simply agree bodily. We have not raised any discourse of arguments of the kind of "pros" and "cons". In fact, we have not focused our conversation on the issue.

[91] Silence application. As usually in these cases, the argument of what is said is not the key question. The argument itself is not usually what we must reason. Our contra-argument, if any, must be constructed to convey a contra-belief. In fact, the proof that the things are as we say is the fact the person we are speaking to does not insist on his argument after our silence, on the contrary he starts another argument, that is, changes the focus of conversation.

[92] We are used to saying that blaming behavior is frequently an auto-exculpatory behavior. Attacking blaming behavior in the context of masked behavior may be considered a "fighting" behavior due to painfully unconfident unconscious feeling. When this painful feeling happens associated with the more unconscious than conscious processing of a cause-effect relationship where the cause is I and the effect is my behavior, then I feel guilty. The response to this painful feeling may be an attacking blaming behavior, which involves compensating auto-exculpatory feeling.

[93] Body language expressing painful feeling. Remember the markers of masked behavior. We are wondering whether so much rage is proportional to the reasons being argued.

[94] She verbally intends to justify her discomfort. The intensity of her painful feeling behavior does not seem proportional to the justifications, which must be considered precipitant causal factors, but not the basic causal factors.

[95] Verbal and body pacing. Response to feeling, but not to masked arguments.

[96] Resistance masked behavior. She continues to express her discomfort.

[97] Resistance masked behavior. She goes on with attacking blaming behavior.

[98] In front of resistance masked behavior, we have no choice. We must continue verbal and body pacing.

Soon, she more quietly resumes her conversation to talk about a different theme[100]. She says again: "I am getting a bit of a belly. I see myself fat". I ask her. "What exactly do you mean?[101]" She answers. "I feel a load in my belly".

INTRODUCTORY WORDS

"Well, what I'm going to explain to you, perhaps[102], you'll find it nonsense and absurd. In fact, surely, it has not to do with you[103]. Do not worry. However, let me say to you what comes to my mind just now. Sometimes, we are convinced that we can control persons, things, actions. But, can you at will have rain stop[104]?"

MASKED HYPOTHETICAL QUESTION

"I am wondering, you know[105], when the teacher asked me to read something, I felt an unpleasant sensation that made me shake so that I was unable to do it". He/she answers: "Yes, yes, that's it"[106].

---

[99] We add silence to verbal and body pacing. We multiply the effect of pacing. We must keep in mind that the masked behavior in its way of "fighting" behavior may turn out provocative (attacking). In fact, this attitude represents an unconscious way to be given a lot of attention. The primitive brain responsible for masked behavior does not process ideas or concepts. It triggers a reactive behavior in order to reach attention because a dangerous signal (may be life threatening) is being processed.

[100] Our previous procedure has an effect. Rage decreases and shift of focus happens again.

[101] Semantic question. This resort is useful to verify how the literal linguistic formulation does not agree with its conceptual meaning. This phenomenon is typical of masked verbal language, which is a consequence of feeling, but not of reflexive thought. As any question, on the other hand, an Ericksonian hypnosis effect is produced.

[102] Hypothetical and ambiguous terms. Remember that this formulation makes its effect by means of the implicit prompting effect. Neurologically and psycholinguistically, this is processed as an experience of choosing or opting-out, that is, decision making in the sense one decides the comment is applicable to oneself. Anyway, what is clear is the person, we are speaking to, feels better than when we use more direct linguistic communication

[103] Masked reference: "…it has not to do with you." This formulation works similarly to hypothetical terms we have already explained. Her we can implicitly see a prompting effect. On the other hand, the non-painful effect is clearly observed.

[104] As you can see, the message we want to communicate is "Sometimes, we are…rain stop?" Instead of saying it directly, we introduce it by using a long introductory discourse where no specific message is intended. All this introductory discourse, where it is not clear the sense or purpose, makes the individual, we are speaking to, be obliged to an effort of concentration (hypnosis effect).

[105] Introductory expression. You can see the application of a resort (masked hypothetical question) involves the combined use of other different resorts.

[106] Here, we can see the answer to a masked question. Instead of formulating a direct question about what is intended, we do it indirectly. The more direct, the more rational, but also the more painful. We claim that the empathic therapeutic effect is based on feeling communication. This indirect way of questioning avoids the painful feeling associated with more direct questioning.

PRESCRIPTION OR SYMPTOM

"Look, I'm sure[107] you are never hungry[108]". She answers with a nod[109]. I continue: "You know, undoubtedly[110], you can't eat unless you have a good appetite. Therefore, you must pay attention to your appetite. It'll say to you if your stomach is ready to digest food. Your appetite will tell you for sure. Then, you'll be able to eat as you like".

METAPHORS AS A PROTOTYPE OF INDIRECT COMMUNICATION AND ERICKSONIAN HYPNOSIS

Metaphor (analogy) is one of the most powerful ways to communicate that man has ever devised; probably one of the oldest, too. But powerful communication between people is much more than just the transfer of information. We can all transfer information towards another person, but making it meaningful and having an impact on that other person is another story. Voice, expressions, words, movements are anchored to good feeling while the metaphor is told. Then, good feeling will emerge whenever the anchor triggers the relationship set up.

HOUSE METAPHOR

"Look, I'm going to draw several things. I must say to you I'm not an expert[111]". I draw a house on a paper on the table while I ask him/her[112]: "Well, this is easy, isn't it? What do you

---

[107] ..."I'm sure"... In applying prescription of symptoms, we must be very confident. This is one of the cases during the procedure when we must be assertive. We must convey we are very convinced both verbally and bodily. Again, we must believe the things work this way, otherwise our body language will contradict our verbal language.

[108] Here the symptom is anorexia. The prescription of symptom consists of verbal pacing in the sense the symptom or behavior is a reactive response to painful feeling. Remember pacing is oriented not to reinforce the masked reactive behavior. Something like a "fight" behavior which are searching for problems, although we must consider it as an attention demand. The anorexic behavior, like any other reactive behavior, will be reinforced whenever the response to the reactive behavior is provoking painful feeling. It is said in neurolinguistic programming that the response which reinforces the behavior is working because of polarity response (opposite effect). That is, I don't want to eat, you force me to eat, so I won't eat. In fact, neurolinguistic programming explanation is a descriptive one, but not a real cause-effect reason. We think our neurologically based explanation has a good rationale.

It must be added that the prescription of symptom has an extraordinary anti-blame effect, when correctly indicated. We must indicate (apply) this resort particularly in resistance behaviors. Under these behaviors, we can find a profound unconscious guilty sentiment. Remember the blame sentiment is the consequence of painful feeling processing associated to a causal-effect relationship processing, where the person is responsible for his/her dysfunctional behavior. The person doing a resistance dysfunctional behavior is usually given the message "behaving this way is not morally correct". We must remark anorexia can be substituted for any other behavior like hyperkinesia, dyslexia, and so on, and the prescription of symptom is likewise applicable successfully.

[109] Body language communication. According to our framework, there is no reason for looking for confirmatory verbal communication. Body language tells us reliably.

[110] Again, we apply what has been explained in point one.

[111] Anticipation and confusion. We say what we are going to do, which avoids uncertainty on the part of our patient. Adding the comment on expertise, we provoke certain confusion because the person we are speaking

think it is about?[113]" Unequivocally, they answer. "A house". I continue my drawing, adding[4] clouds and lightning to the picture while[114] I'm telling a tale. Generally, children pay attention and show an expectant face[115]. Next, I ask[116] them: "What do you think will happen to the house with this fiercely bad weather?" They always answer. "It will be ruined".

Then, near the house, I draw a little man as I say: "Well, this is me when I was your age." And I add: "I am going to tell you how my life was passing day by day. Can you imagine how the day began[117]? "Usually, children look at me with a surprised face[118]. Immediately, I continue[119]: "First of all, the alarm clock rings. Do you believe I get up?[120]". The surprise increases. More than less frequently, the answer is "yes", although sometimes with a questioning tone of voice. I answer. "No, I was a little lazy"[121]. This is followed by a more or less openly smiling face of the person I'm speaking to[122]. I go on: "Then, a voice came to me and said you must[123] get up, come on, get up!". Simultaneously[124], I draw a lightning going to

---

to usually expects to find an expert in every matter. Don't forget confusion contributes to Ericksonian hypnosis.

[112] Channels saturation is one of our purposes because it contributes to Ericksonian hypnosis. We are drawing and simultaneously talking.

[113] Soon, we resort to question application. Remember the hypnotic effect and the prompting effect.

[114] Saturation of channels is pursued. the more information is provided to each channel, the more saturation is produced.

[115] Body language feedback tells us about attention and feeling. Of course, body language tells us about resistance behavior.

[116] Question application continues.

[117] Saturation of channels is continuously practiced as well as questions are constantly formulated.

[118] Body language feedback illustrative of confusion.

[119] Without pause, the discourse goes on to take advantage of the confusion state and hence to keep successfully Ericksonian hypnosis.

[120] Question application looking for confusion once again.

[121] Confusion is kept on.

[122] Body language feedback.

[123] We are making the child cognitively process the informative content of the metaphor, which will be internalized and transferred to his/her own context, with the associated feeling. Ordinarily, any cognitive content that is processed, internalized, and transferred is compared to the previous knowledge (knowledge base) the person has. Forming the knowledge base, everybody has his/her beliefs. Beliefs determine self-concept and self-steem, and self-confident (self-feeling). Taking into account the masked painful unconfident behavior is unconsciously processed and therefore the painful unconfident feeling is generally unconsciously processed, the first objective in therapy or education is to make the person be aware that he/she is feeling badly. Secondly, that his/her painful feeling is a consequence of something happening outside himself / herself. This implies the cause-effect relationship is put between an external cause beyond me and my feeling, but not between an internal cause (I / me) and my feeling, which involves blame sentiment. As you can see, this mental process we are referring to, according to which we make an unconscoius information become conscious in order to positively change the belief that then will be re-memorized, is the same mental process that takes place in PASS planning training.

As a last resort, this mental process influences personal beliefs in the sense that it determines the processing of "I am not guilty". Again, the feeling processing is the target we pursue.

We practice three kinds of metaphor from less to most affecting. First, the non-personal metaphor, where the therapist is not present. Second, the personal metaphor, where the therapist is the protagonist. And third, the personal ask-for-help metaphor, where the therapist is the protagonist and furthermore is asking the patient for help. The metaphor we have just told must be considered a personal metaphor. By the way, the impact factor of the therapist communication in general may be classified according to this previous rank.

Note that the more linked to the context of the patient the metaphor is about, the more easy the transference happens. Concerning the metaphor above, we can see that its matter is present in everybody's life. Don't forget metaphor is a prototypical application of concrete processing according to what we have already explained about conducted Ericksonian hypnosis.

the head of my little man on the paper. I proceed: "Eventually, I get up and sleepily take a shower." The voice came back to say: " Come on, you must[125] hurry, you must[125] have breakfast!" Later on, the voice returned again and again: "You have to[126] get ready to go to school. You must … You have to…" As soon as I was at school, another voice was saying: "You must…you have to…" Every "you must", "you have to", is accompanied by[127] a lightning to the head on the paper. Then, pointing to[128] the head of my little man, I say: "What do you believe may happen to the head?" Unanimously, they say: "It may be hurt or damaged or something like that"[129]. Next we practice amnesia. An excellent way of practicing amnesia is to follow through with another metaphor.

CHEST OF DRAWERS METAPHOR

I draw a chest of drawers having three drawers, a top one, a bottom one, and another between them in the middle. I say: "When I was your age, I had this idea. I said to myself I'll put every *I must* or *I have to* in the upper drawer, every *I want* in the lower drawer, and every *I like* in the middle[130]." I am writing *I must, I have to, I want,* and *I like* near the appropriate drawer. As I am referring to the upper drawer, I draw lightning[131] while I am saying "I must get up", "I have to go to school", "I must take care of…", and so on. And I go on as follows: "I do not know about you[132], but my upper drawer was so full as to have 40 kg, the drawer in the middle, may be, 4 kg, and the lower one 1 kg at the most". Next, I add: "What do you think can happen to this furniture with so much weight in the top[133]?" Invariably, they respond. "It will break". I proceed: "And[134]…, what could[135] we do to prevent it?" Some keep quiet looking for an answer, as their eyes[136] show us the processing being used, Others respond what they believe would be a solution. Here, I propose the solution: "Look, may be[137], a good solution would[8] be to transfer from the top into the bottom, because the weight

---

[124] Saturation of channels by making visual and auditive information be processed simultaneously.

[125] The verbal communication reinforces the message according to which an external factor (you must / you have to) may justify painful feeling.

[126] At this point, previous reinforcement continues.

[127] Again, we practice saturation of channels as we have just set out in point fourteen.

[128] We continue to practice saturation of channels.

[129] Verbal feedback informing of mental processing.

[130] Saturation of channels and its effect we have already explained.

[131] Anchoring effect. Ordinarily, we explain this metaphor after "the house metaphor". This means that what we are telling and drawing here is directly connected (associated) with what we told and drew there. Therefore, the same message is implicitly conveyed by this procedure.

[132] This is an example of masked question. Although we don't ask directly, the brain of the person listening to us is driven to say it.

[133] As usual, question application is a rule.

[134] This formulation, where we initiate a statement and immediately discontinue the discourse with an expecting silence while we are thinking, has a high impacting factor for Ericksonian hypnosis. The person we are speaking to remains waiting for something.

[135] Here we combine hypothetical term with question application.

[136] The body language feedback informs us of the cognitive processing pattern being used by our patient. Remember eye pattern allows us to infer what PASS processing is being used. This is a useful information for us to formulate our messages.

[137] Again, hypothetical terms.

will be better supported by the furniture[138]". Then, I add: "I was just wondering[139] if you know someone who *wants* what he/she does not *like*.[140] Do you know?[141]" I do not wait for an answer. I proceed: "Really, I do not know anybody. In fact, at this moment, I am remembering[142] my family[143] was on an occasion invited to a wedding. All the children were located around a table full of food, chocolate, and so on. I must say to you I like[144] chocolate very much. I am crazy about it. A waitress came up to us and said we could eat whatever we wish. Nobody moved. The waitress insisted again. Then, I began eating so much chocolate that I was about to throw up. But[145]..., do you know what happened later[146]? I did not think what could come afterwards[147]. That night, I was suffering[148] from diarrhea and a bellyache.

---

[138] Here is the message. The top purpose of the message is always the personal belief scope. As we have already said As a rule, any cognitive content that is processed, internalized, and transferred is compared to the previous knowledge (knowledge base) the person has. Forming the knowledge base, everybody has his/her beliefs. Beliefs determine self-concept and self-steem, and self-confident (self-feeling). Remember that the first objective in therapy or education is to make the person be aware that he/she is feeling badly, because masked behavior is unconsciously processed. Additionally, that his/her painful feeling is a consequence of something happening outside himself / herself. This is an anti-blame sentiment effect and has a bearing on personal beliefs. This communication is partially due to anchorage effect we have mentioned above. The cognitive informative message we are communicating here to be consciously processed is moreover that the experience "I must / I have to" may cause devastating feeling effect on us. The better condition is the "I want". Later on, we will complete the message to make clear the pathologic "I must / I have to", and the meaning of "I like / I want." But don't forget. Every message in this procedure has an effect; however the golden rule is that we help to change personal identity on the base of personal experiences of decision making and unconditional support that produce inductive cognitive - feeling learning. Note that this is a personal metaphor, according to the classification we have established. And likewise remember that metaphor is a prototypical application of concrete processing according to what we have already explained about conducted Ericksonian hypnosis.

[139] Introductory phrase contributing to Eericksonian hypnosis.

[140] The message goes on here. The knowledge we state now is what "I like" and "I want" means. Note that the concept is "I have to / I must" means the behavior driven by the impulse as an uncontrolled overreacting behavior, which involves unpleasant painful feeling. Instead, "I want" means decision making not being influenced by driven uncontrolled impulse. In usual linguistic terms, the moral obligation must be linked to "I want". The practice of "I want" implies the assessment of consequences and their feeling. Although the practice of "I want" is oriented to reach a final pleasant consequence, the immediate or intermediate consequences needed to reach the final consequence may be unpleasant. This knowledge is involved in "I like" versus "I want". These cognitive statements may be translated into beliefs according to the formula "A is / has B". For instance, "have to / must" is an uncontrolled impulse. Once this is internalized and transferred, a personal extrapolation takes place automatically. "I am impulsive if I behave according to 'I have / I must'". If the person we are speaking to processes this way, then a painful mental process happens. Indirect communication technique makes this process be less painful. If less painful, then more pleasant and furthermore less resistance masked behavior. Don't forget that the golden rule is that we help to change personal identity on the basis of personal experiences of decision making and unconditional support that produce inductive cognitive - feeling learning.

[141] Question application.

[142] Next we practice amnesia by resorting to an excellent way of practicing amnesia which is to follow through with another metaphor.

[143] We introduce another personal metaphor that as you will remember is more impacting than non-personal one.

[144] Here continues the message. We are teaching "I like" versus "I want". "I want" takes into account the final consequences, not assessing exclusively the immediate consequences, but "I like" just assesses the immediate result of a decision.

[145] Expecting silence is practiced here.

[146] Questions are used again and again.

[147] The message is resumed here, insisting on the importance of assessing the final consequence from the point of view of feeling.

[148] Final painful feeling as a consequence is highlighted here.

It was awful, I cannot forget it". Without stopping, I continue[149]: "You know, imagine the most evil monster in the world. He comes in, just here, stands up before the door to prevent us from running away, and says you and I have to do something we do not like[150]. Can you make rain stop[151]? I do not know anybody who can make the rain stop when raining. I do not know what you would do[152], but I would do something, the least I could do, in order to try getting out safely. I would not forget what comes afterwards[153].

BACKPACK METAPHOR

"My parents, brother, and sister were used to riding a bike. Each one carried his/her backpack over the shoulders. However, something curious occurred. Do you know what?[154]". I do not wait for an answer and continue to say: "My mother used to put my mac in her backpack, and my father put the mac of my sister in his packback. Usually, I, my brother, and my father rode faster than my mother and sister, such that we agreed to ride at our own pace, doing the outing in stages. One day, it began raining and suddenly water was pouring down. Unfortunately, my mac was not there in my backpack. My sister found herself without her mac that was in father's backpack[155]".

---

[149] Another metaphor is introduced here to make amnesia post-trance.

[150] The message is resumed again to teach how a rational decision making takes into account the final consequence in terms of feeling, although the immediate consequence is not pleasant. Additionally, another relevant knowledge is conveyed: sometimes we can't avoid the immediate unpleasant consequence because we can decide what we can but not what is beyond our possibility. We can decide what depends on us, but not what doesn't. Remember we had taught incorrect decision making with final unpleasant consequence, but immediate pleasant consequence.

[151] The message is rounded off.

[152] Masked question application.

[153] The most relevant knowledge in the message is highlighted. But don't forget that the golden rule is that we help to change personal identity on the base of personal experiences of decision making and unconditional support, which produces inductive cognitive - feeling learning.

[154] This is a personal metaphor versus non-personal one. Note that indirect communication demands a long phrase, clause, and sentence, in the sense of rhetorical effect. This formulation demands a higher attention effort based on working memory that, we know, has a limited capacity beyond a limit. Remember that this implies Ericksonian hypnosis effect. As a rule, we practice questions as soon as we see the opportunity.

[155] Every metaphor includes a message, namely, knowledge to be confronted with the knowledge base of the person we are speaking to. The general belief here is "decision making is what everybody needs, instead non-decision making may be painful."The golden rule is that we help to change personal identity on the basis of personal experiences of decision making and unconditional support, which produces inductive cognitive - feeling learning. Communicating this learning is a first step, but the success is in creating a favorable context for him/her to live experiences of decision making and unconditional support. In creating an adequate context, we practice the systemic psychological therapy [Minuchin, 1974; Madanes, 1985] as an excellent resort, although always according to our theoretical framework. Prompting individual decision making raises the issue of discipline and learning of limits. We claim that even punishment following discipline break-up can be in advance decided (making a pact) between parents and children and between teachers and pupils, at least from as soon as 5 or 7 years old. We'll return to that.

PATHWAYS METAPHOR

"I would like[156] to tell you something that happened in my[157] home sometimes. My mother had something to discuss with my father[158]. Instead of approaching him, she came to me, and angrily told me how she was upset about him. I did not understand anything. In fact, I wondered why she was telling that to me. Also, my father behaved the same way sometimes. I was confused again, without understanding what was happening. To make matters worse, my mother or father sometimes came to me to scold me, but not mentioning one to another. Really, I[159] felt badly!"

KNOCKING-BEFORE-COMING IN METAPHOR

"When I[160] was your age[161], I had the idea I am going to tell you[162]. I was overwhelmed with constant orders so that I decided[163] to take a paper, write on it *please, knock before coming in*, and stick it on the door of my room. As soon as my mother came to my room, she saw the notice on the door, tore the paper into tiny bits, and shouted at me a telling-off. I did not know what to do. I said to myself it was not as bad as all that[164]. Next day I did not dare to repeat my action, but I did it days later. This time, my father came to me and told me off, warning me I would be punished for doing it again. The paper suffered the same fate as before. I remained stunned during the next days. But something internally drove me to do it again and again. Sometimes my mother, other times my father, or many times both of them came to my room and the show came to life again and again. One day, something unexpected happened. I put the paper on the door, nobody said anything[165], I went to school, I came back from it, and the paper remained stuck on the door. A week passed without incident when I myself decided[166] to remove the much talked-about paper".

---

[156] Hypothetical terms application.

[157] Again, an example of personal metaphor.

[158] Here is the message. The knowledge and associated feeling to be processed is "my feeling (thereof my behavior) may be a consequence of external causal factors (even my parents)". This will become a non-personal belief once it is internalized and transferred, and immediately will become a personal belief. The extrapolation to personal belief: "If I am not a causal factor, I am not guilty".

[159] The personal component of the metaphor is closely linked to feeling.

[160] Again, a personal metaphor is utilized here.

[161] Context approach.

[162] Introductory words application.

[163] Here is the message of this metaphor. As already mentioned, first of all, the transference of what we are communicating is easier when the context of the patient is related to the context of the metaphor. By the way, we must remark that the more similar the content is, the more easy the transference is, such that the more easy, the less Ericksonian hypnosis happens because attention effort is reduced to a minimum. The message is "decision making is normal independent of the age". This corresponds to a non-personal belief that will be extrapolated into personal belief: " I am normal, if I make decisions".

[164] The message is complemented with the knowledge: "a behavior disproportional to the causes is a non-sense behavior."

[165] Here the previous commented message is reinforced.

[166] Here, reinforcement of point four.

WHAT-ARE-YOU-DOING AND SIX-MONTHS-OLD-BABY METAPHORS

A 3-year-old[167] child carrying some toys, his mother, and a mother's friend walk in single file. Suddenly, the little boy runs into something and noisily falls. He does not cry. On hearing the noise, the mother and the mother's friend turn around. The exaggeratedly[168] scared mother with frightening[169] body and paraverbal language shouts: what's up? The little boy starts crying[170]. Then the mother's friend asks: why does he cry? She answers[171]: he fell. Well, what I have just told you makes me recall the following I experienced just here[172]. A 6-month-old infant[173] is taken to my office by her parents and her grandmother. She is laid on my office table in horizontal posture, her grandmother stands by near to the table, her parents sit down in front of me. Suddenly, the infant intends to sit up[174]. Practically he can not get hurt. The grandmother does not move, but the father swiftly goes to the table and with his hands helps the infant to sit up[175]. Then, I ask him: what was up! He answers: he may fall[176].

I continue by saying: "I am wondering[177] how the little boy and the infant will have memorized their experience[178]. I am afraid[179] that every time the little boy behaves doing something that provokes pain to his mother, his mother unconsciously will trigger an overreaction as a consequence more of her past experiencing than of the immediate fact[180]. If so, again and again this mother will be conveying (and the boy will be experiencing) a message we can formulate in terms of 'I am unable / I do badly'. This way, the 'I am not able / I feel badly / I feel unconfident / I am guilty ' may be unconsciously building inside[181]." I go

---

[167] Here is a non-personal metaphor. The protagonist's age is part of the message: "as young as three years is an age enough to happen what we will tell."

[168] The message here is "an exaggerating - overreacting behavior is a consequence of painful unconfident feeling not directly related to the precipitant causal factor." Taking into account the little boy did not get hurt, mother's behavior must be considered an overreacting behavior, a disproportional behavior in terms of cause-effect relationship. If so, her behavior must be considered basically a consequence of a highly over-sensitive felt internal condition (personal identity) coming from the experienced past, the little boy's accident being just a triggering factor.

[169] The message: "the frightening body language is processed even by a 3-year-old child."

[170] The message: "what makes the child cry is not the verbal language, but the para-verbal language, which is as a 'fighting' behavior."

[171] The message: "the verbal behavior is not according to the reality." The thinking brain produces an afterthought. In front of the question, it analyzes quickly what is entering her senses, that is, the experience taking place outside in real time. To elaborate the answer, the thinking brain resorts to previous accumulated - memorized knowledge. In this case, for instance, "a little boy who falls may be injured and subsequently cry".We have utilized this metaphor to illustrate the mechanism of production of masked behavior on neurological base in the chapter dealing this theme.

[172] Amnesia post-trance through another metaphor following the previous one.

[173] Again, a non-personal metaphor. As above, the protagonist's age is part of the message.

[174] The message: "a behavior may be consequence of basic cause plus precipitant cause." The baby sitting up is a precipitant cause, but not the basic cause.

[175] The message: "overprotection may be a consequence of uncontrolled driven behavior."

[176] The message: "the verbal behavior is not according to the reality."

[177] Application of introductory words.

[178] The message: "the personal experience is decisive for building the personal beliefs."

[179] Hypothetical term formulation.

[180] The message here: "the basic cause is not the precipitant cause."

[181] The message to be learned is: "an experience is a learning; a learnt knowledge is a non-personal belief and a personal belief is learnt from a non-personal belief. Also: "the personal beliefs are the reason for our behavior and the blame sentiment is according to the following." Blame sentiment experience is the painful feeling

on this way: "On the other hand, I am afraid[182] that every time the 6-month-old infant intends to do something by herself (sit up, walking, and so on) and memorize "I am able / I am confident / I feel well and confident", her father, who is constantly seeing more danger than expected, will overreact overprotecting[183] and preventing her from experiencing a confident-constructive belief". Next, I practice amnesia post-trance[184].

MAKING A PACT / DISCIPLINE LEARNING

Ivan, 15 years of age, came to our office due to behavioral dysfunction. Interviewing his father, he says to me: "I am desperate. Every weekend, my son is coming back later and later. I am afraid that he gets into serious problems". I answer. "I see. Well, I am going, if you like[185], to explain to you something that comes to my mind exactly now[186]. Let[187] me tell you. Perhaps[188], you'll find this to be nonsense or absurd. Even, maybe, it is not useful for you[189]. In fact, if you find it inappropriate, forget it[190].. You may[191] try this approach. Choose a calm day and talk to him in terms of: Ivan I would[192] like to talk to you about the weekends. This issue is getting worse and worse. I and you are suffering unfortunately. What can we[193] do to solve this problem? "The father listened to me carefully. Next, I anticipated[194] from him that

---

processing associated with a cause - effect relationship where the person experimenting this sentiment processes "I am not doing well, correctly. I am responsible for", making the personal causal-effect responsibility into causal-effect culpability (moral guilt). This unconscious-implicit mental process is happening continuously such that the experience of "doing wrong" tends to be implicitly processed as that of "doing morally wrong". This painful processing is extraordinarily devastating from the point of view of personal identity, self-confidence, self-steem, and so on.

[182] Hypothetical term formulation.

[183] The message now: "overprotecting behavior may be due to a reactive response to personal unconfident painful feeling." Remember that every message is a knowledge to be confronted with the personal knowledge base, it must be internalized and transferred, which implies the person is aware of it, namely, he/she becomes conscious.

[184] As a rule, amnesia post-trance puts the icing on the cake.

[185] Hypothetical term application.

[186] Introductory words instead of going directly to the key message.

[187] Again, hypothetical term formulation.

[188] Again, the previous formulation.

[189] Masked reference (masked negation): " it is not useful for you" This formulation works similarly to hypothetical terms we have already explained. Here, we can implicitly see a prompting effect.

[190] The effect explained in point five is reinforced now.

[191] Again, hypothetical term.

[192] A new hypothetical term. We must remark this profusion in hypothetical terms is indicated basically when a resistance masked behavior may be expected. We are dealing with a thorny issue that, we know, provokes resistance. The non-personal belief "discipline is parents' responsibility" and its personal belief "I am guilty if I do not have responsibility for my son/daughter" poses a high impacting effect on personal identity of everyone.

[193] This is a typical example of the use of "I / we" instead of "you". In particular, this is a case of "we" use instead of "you". Every linguistic term is a cognitive content associated with its sensitive feeling that is neurologically processed. Psycholinguistaclly speaking, we know "you" is processed by the recipient with a more intense feeling component than "we". Dealing with painful feeling, the use of "we" is preferable to "you" for obvious reasons.

[194] Anticipation is also very important in this situation to try guaranteeing the success. This anticipation will make the father not react painfully as to put in action masked contra-behavior.

his son would reject[195] any approach to solve the problem as can be expected because of an immature personality. This rejection would be even provocative[196]. If so, he should be around[197] and try again later. When possible, he should bring up the following: "Ivan, I would like[198] you to come back before one o'clock at night. What can we do[199]?" As predicted, Ivan angrily refused to talk about it. The father followed the plan. He accepted[200] verbally and bodily his behavior. He did not insist on it, but tried it later on again. When the time had come, Ivan said: "OK, father, I will come back at two o'clock at night if you agree". The father, previously instructed by me, agreed as soon as Ivan, for the first time, agreed to compromise[201] with his father. He did not like two o'clock but agreed.

Next week, the father came to my office. As soon as he saw me, he told me: "unbelievable! For the first time in months, Ivan came back at two o'clock at night. Not so good, but better than before." And he added: "But what surprised me most was what he said to me the next morning. He said: "Father, it was a real bugger! At two o'clock I was impelled to come back, I could not avoid looking at my wristwatch[202]."

The next step is to get them to make a pact on the consequences if the pact is broken[203]. Even this negative aspect is susceptible to be agreed and the experience says to us that everybody tends to take the consequences that have been mutually agreed upon.

LEARNING AND BEHAVIORAL DYSFUNCTION

Case 1

Victor, a 13-year-old boy is being treated because of learning difficulties and behavioral dysfunction. His tutor[204] comes to see me and tells me that Victor has verbally threatened a

---

[195] We foresee the reactive behavior of his son, as can be expected given that his son is doing masked unconfident painful behavior, which we have previously diagnosed.

[196] The masked behavior is a behavior oriented to take attention. In neurological terms, this is logical because the masked behavior is due to painful reaction, but not to reflexive thinking activity. Things happen as if the brain processing pain and insecurity but not thoughts triggered a response in the sense of taking the attention in order for someone to do something because a dangerous situation is occurring. This requirement of attention may become provocative. Anyway, the masked behavior is a profitable conduct in the sense the masked behavior is followed by some contra-behavior giving compensating benefit. This action-reaction interaction happens in the familiar context, and other different contexts like school, etc. That's why systemic analysis [Minuchin, 1974; Madanes, 1985] and subsequent intervention oriented to break up this interaction becomes crucial in many occasions.

[197] Here, we are dealing with pacing.

[198] Hypothetical term application.

[199] Question application. Again the typical use of "we" instead of "you". See above.

[200] Pacing application.

[201] Compromise involves making decision.

[202] To reach a compromise over something involves a painful blame sentiment if the compromise is broken. So far, this evidence has been widely verified in psychological terms. Neurologically, any decision experience is linked to a personal belief in the sense of "I have responsibility for my decision and therefore I am morally correct if I am consistent with my decision". What makes this processing be felt this way probably has to do with the feeling the 'culture' (values) assigns to an experience like decision making.

[203] Indeed, even this discipline aspect can be agreed according to the procedure we are explaining.

North African classmate with killing him. The tutor is hopeless and furious, and argues she can't say and do anything to change the behavior of Victor[205]. She adds that she wants to help him, but she is unable to find how to do it. I suggest[206] to her that she has a talk with him in an appropriate relaxed time in terms of "I" instead of "you", complementing in terms of "what can we do to solve this"[207]. For instance: "Victor, I am worried. I do not like what has happened. I feel badly[208]. What can we do to solve this?" Next week, her tutor comes to see me and tells me that she is surprised. Victor, she says, reacted quite well. He did not refuse my conversation and we ended up with an agreement[209] according to which he would go out of the classroom five minutes whenever he was nervous enough to create a problem. Since then, when I see he is getting nervous, I do an agreed signal and he spontaneously leaves the classroom, coming back minutes later. Fortunately, things are improving.

Case 2

David, a 14-year-old boy is being treated because of aggressive behavior in the classroom. He has been quarreling with a classmate and comes to see me. As soon as I see him, I ask him how he is doing. He does not answer, looks down[210], and shows watery eyes[211]. I touch[212] his shoulder and say him: "Sometimes, we feel badly[213]". He does not say anything. I continue: "When I[214] was little, sometimes I quarreled and then I felt so badly[215]!"

---

[204] Who is making the demand? Who is suffering? Ordinarily, who makes the demand is worried and therefore is under painful feeling processing. If so, who is demanding help may be doing masked behavior. This doesn't seem the case.

[205] Remember the criteria for diagnosing masked behavior. The "hopeless and furious" behavior must be analyzed according to the criteria.

[206] Hypothetical term application.

[207] Application of "I / we" instead of "you". Remember that every linguistic term is a cognitive content associated with its sensitive feeling that is neurologically processed. Psycholinguistically speaking, we know "you" is processed by the recipient with a more intense feeling component than "we" and "I". Dealing with painful feeling, the use of "we" and "I" are preferable to "you" for obvious reasons.

[208] This is an example of ask-for-help formulation. This is an "I am worried / I am badly" formulation. This kind of expression implicitly involves a masked asking-for-help situation. In some way, this attitude is equivalent to a submission posture in front of a fighting behavior in animal conduct. This may be considered a pacing resort that avoids polarity reaction in neurolinguistic terms. At this point, we must recall this resort of communication has a high impacting effect.

[209] This is a particular case of "making a pact" that we have explained above.

[210] Body language informing of painful feeling. Remember this attitude may be considered a "flight" behavior.

[211] Again, body language tells us about painful feeling. Don't forget that even the painful behavior may be assessed in terms of masked behavior. The markers (criteria) we explained about masked behavior must be looked for. There is a difference between masked and non-masked crying behavior. The masked crying behavior is unconsciously processed such that the crying act appears theatrical. The non-masked crying behavior is consciously processed and therefore it implies conscious suffering.

[212] Touching application contributes to Ericksonian hypnosis by means of channels saturation and pattern break-up of information processing. Furthermore, touching is body language communicating feeling, which is at this moment associated (anchored) with what we say next about sentiments.

[213] Verbal language communication about feeling reinforcing (anchoring) the previous body language. As above in point three, we are practicing pacing. Note that the response as a therapist to the state of our patient is focussed on feeling, but, don't forget, in the sense of "I am aware of your painful feeling and therefore I regret your suffering". This is pacing. Paradoxically, sometimes somebody in good faith copes with this suffering person saying "don't worry" associated with a trivializing body language. This is not pacing.

[214] Now a personal metaphor begins.

David looks up at me[216]. I go on: "Look, it happened as if a force drove me to do something, and then I can't control my doing[217]". He answers me that the same is for him[218]. I add: "You know, it happens as if the others would know which switch to touch for us to uncontrollably respond[219] ". He answers yes with a nod[220]. I ask him where that switch is[221]. He remains silent but thinking, and next he softly says: "On my inside". I touch[222] his shoulder and I go on: "Look, if you like[223], right now you could close your eyes[224] and try and see the switch[225]". David easily closes his eyes, breathes deeply, and relaxes[226]. I continue: "David can see the switch inside, can't he?" He answers. "Yes, yes, it is inside my belly". I add: "What color[227]?" He goes on: "It is red and very easy to set up!" I say: "OK, David, we get it. Do you like that it works so easily?[228] "He answers: "No, of course!" I say: "Look, do you know what we can do[229]? If you like[230], you can put a protective cover[231] so that it was needed to lift the cover to get to set up the switch". He remains with closed eyes and responds yes with a nod[232]. Body language feedback tells me he is relaxed and immediately I shift the focus of conversation to another theme[233]. I ask him about his sport activities. For instance: "By the way, David, now I don't remember if you practice football. Do you?"

---

[215] The message is the non-personal belief "quarrelling is painful feeling". Quarrelling is consciously lived as compensating pleasant experience in the sense of tension release, whereas it is unconsciously processed as a suffering state, which, in fact, triggers the quarrelling behavior. As soon as "quarrelling is painful feeling" is made conscious, the transference to personal belief happens in terms of " I feel badly".

[216] Body language feedback of eye contact indicating an excellent response to our intervention.

[217] The message continues: "some behaviors are uncontrollable"

[218] Verbal language feedback of transference: "I am an uncontrollable behavior child", then "I am morally correct".

[219] The message goes on: "some behaviors are due to external provocative acts".

[220] Body language feedback of transference: "external causes are provocative", then "I am not responsible for".

[221] A conducted process of Ericksonian hypnosis is started here in order to make a relaxing effect. We resort to concrete-tangible knowledge: "the switch". Re-read what we said about directed Ericksonian hypnosis.

[222] An application of anchoring (touching) at the right moment. See point three. This procedure reinforces feeling processing.

[223] Note we have formulated hypothetical terms.

[224] To avoid distractor effect.

[225] Immediately, we return to "the switch", the concrete-tangible knowledge we are using to symbolically represent the "voluntary control" on the behavior.

[226] Body language feedback of relaxing effect.

[227] We proceed making our patient saturate the channels of information with concrete-tangible data content regarding vision and so on. Remember the Ericksonian hypnosis effect that follows.

[228] Question application to reinforce Ericksonian hypnosis effect.

[229] Here more questions. Furthermore, "we" formulation instead of "you". Again, remember the effect that produces this resort.

[230] Hypothetical term.

[231] We continue to use symbolic concrete-tangible terms to imagine (mentally live) a pleasant relaxing experience.

[232] Body language feedback informing us that we are doing well.

[233] The amnesia post-trance application puts an end.

Case 3

A teacher[234] comes to see me and says that Jordi, a 15-year-old boy, is getting worse and worse. He is always disturbing his classmates and teachers, and takes a couldn't-care-less attitude. The teacher[234] asks me for help. She makes Jordi come to see me. I introduce[235] myself to him, and I say to him that his teacher has come to talk with me about him. I add that I am going to explain to him what she said to me[236], and that, maybe, the things are not exactly that way, but that it is her version. I tell him and he agrees the things are going that way. Then, I say: "What do you mean[237]?" Silence. Next, he continues[238]: "Well, whenever somebody picks on me, I hit him". I go on: "Look, Jordi, do you know what I make of it[239]?" He remains attentive. I continue: "I guess your father thinks that we have to defend oneself against aggressors by always using force[240]". He immediately says: "Indeed, once or twice I came back home crying because I had been hit on my face. My father told me that next time somebody hit me, he himself would also hit me for being stupid". I say: "Right, I see. You should feel so badly[241]!" He keeps quiet and sad[242]. I add: [243] "When I was little, one day I saw a group of children pulling down my motorbike. I was furious, but can you make rain stop[244]? I was not able to do anything but doing nothing. I wanted to feel myself well afterwards. Later, I thought about what I could do to avoid that situation again, if possible[245]". Instead, a friend of mine found himself in a similar situation. He thought he was a chicken if he did nothing so he get into a quarrel and his right arm was broken[246]. I add: "Do you think I

---

[234] Who is making the demand? Who is suffering? Remember that who makes the demand is worried and therefore is under painful feeling processing. If so, who is demanding help may be doing masked behavior.

[235] Anticipation and subtle application of prompting. As we have already explained, there is anticipation because in so far as I introduce myself; my patient can foresee what is coming, which releases tension and fear. Any painful-fearful factor plays against our purpose. However, not only this effect is produced, but also we are subtly making our patient experience autonomy in the sense his/her brain processes how he/she individually copes with a particular situation.

[236] Again subtle application of prompting in the same sense above exposed.

[237] Semantic question. Remember that this question allows us to verify how the literal linguistic formulation does not agree with its conceptual meaning. This is typical of masked verbal language, which is a consequence of feeling, but not of reflexive thinking. On the other hand, any question produces an ericksonian hypnosis effect.

[238] Remember that the silence must be applied being aware of not provoking discomfort to the person I am speaking to. We call this silence a productive silence in the sense that our silence is always followed by a resuming initiative of the other.

[239] Question application.

[240] Message of a non-personal belief (knowledge + feeling) determining a personal belief. We are making him be aware of a belief we are going to argue next in order to change the meaning and the associated feeling.

[241] Verbal linguistic pacing that dialogs with feeling, forgetting linguistic content of the other.

[242] Body language feedback of feeling.

[243] The message goes on.

[244] The message is "being well is the purpose wanted" and "decision making is to think consequences". We are teaching and he is learning.

[245] Teaching work continues: "prevention is sometimes necessary".

[246] The teaching message focuses on the consequences.

was a chicken[247]?" Surprised[248], he look at me and says: "No!" I ask him about the last football match[249]

---

[247] Change of belief (knowledge + feeling). Application of question with the hypnotic effect we have already explained.

[248] Body language feedback.

[249] Amnesia post-trance.

Chapter 7

OVERVIEW AND CONCLUSION

The aim of this final chapter is to summarize the basic points of the previous chapter in order to clarify what it is about. In essence, we are dealing with a model to diagnose and treat dysfunctional behaviors, the foundation of which is based on neurological reasons.

METHODOLOGICAL FRAMEWORK

In chapter one, we raised the question of research methodology. This procedure has been constructed resorting to a method of investigation. We have used both quantitative and qualitative research.

Quantitative investigation has been basically utilized for cognitive investigation. Within the quantitative method, the multivariate analysis, in particular, principal component factorial analysis as a maximum likelihood method of extraction and VARIMAX rotation has been relevant for factorial analysis. Usual tests widely used for assessing differences between both means and proportions, as well as correlations were successfully applied. Also, cluster analysis proved to be a useful tool. Qualitative investigation [Jones, 1995; Mays & Pope, 1995, Greenhalgh & Taylor, 1997; Green & Britten, 1998; Crabtree & Miller, 1992; Creswell, 1994] has been applied to study dysfunctional behaviors.

Concerning qualitative research, we have described in detail the method we have been following, stressing the fact that the procedure has been normalized and published [Perez-Alvarez & Timoneda, 1998; Mayoral-Rodríguez, 2002; Alabau-Bofill, 2003] in order for anyone to be able to replicate the study.

We must emphasize that the sample we have qualitatively studied is considerable (N = 1333) and although limitations can be argued, validity and reliability to guarantee results and conclusions excluding the chance or placebo effect are reasonable. On the other hand, we must remember that quantitative research is not free of limitations [Ionnidis, 2005].

The fMRI methodology is explained in detail in the chapter on our research. We have intended to expose as clearly as possible how seeing what the neurons do allows us to infer what the behaviors mean. A major goal of our research has been to tally what external observation of behavior tells us with what the neurons do.

This chapter on methodology ends with a comment on casualty concept [Balmes, 1968, Shand, 2000]. Scientifically speaking, the aim of any study on behavior is to discover the cause of the behavior. We recall that a cause is something that determines another something as a necessary and sufficient condition or, if multiple conditions are involved, as each necessary and jointly sufficient condition. We musn't forget that we must identify the first cause in a chain of causes, and, on the other hand, to differentiate a precipitant non-necessary non-sufficient causal factor from an essential necessary sufficient factor. This approach is very crucial in order to plan a successful intervention.

NEUROBIOLOGICAL CONCEPT OF BEHAVIOR

In chapter two, we bring up a discussion on the concept of neurobiological behavior. Behavior must be neuro-biologically considered in any external manifestation in a human being whatsoever. This is not really the usual sense of this term. Our concept has to do with the central processing of information concept that we will deal with in the next chapter [Das 2003, Das et al, 1994, 1996, 2000]. The key is that information is processed entering (input) via sensorial input, whether visual, auditory or kinesthetic, and leaving (output) either verbal or non-verbal. The behavior is outside, but the central processing is inside. What matters is what happens at the central level.

This concept of behavior has been studied from different fields of science, including philosophy [Balmes, 1964], anthropology [Bateson, 1979], psychology[Das, 2003; Das et al, 1994, 1996, 2000], neurology [Lamote de Grignon, 1993], and neuroscience [LeDoux, 1996].

Traditionally, mind and brain have been dissociated by arguing the brain is a noisy organ which is very difficult to interpret. However, we must admit that the mind is supported by the brain. Nowadays, we are more than starting to see how the neurons work. The cognitive mental process has practically always been accepted, but the feeling mental process has been considered difficult to approach, much too intangible. However, the most recent neuroimaging investigation is throwing light on the shadow. At present, it is unacceptable to reject the assumption that under every behavior there is both cognition and emotion.

Science has been also classically worried about cognitive assessment as far as achievement is concerned. Pursuing this aim, psychometry developed and intelligence became a static value instead of a dynamic value. But the reality is that the cognitive concept is far from being unequivocally defined. If we have not defined it, then we'll have problems trying to study it. Consequently, the results will be difficult to interpret.

In this sense, the PASS theory of intelligence [Das 2003; Das et al. 1994, 1996, 2000] means a new view. Its foundation is based on Luria's neurological lesion studies [Luria, 1980: Das, 1999a]. This means its framework is different from those previous theories of intelligence. Therefore, the DN:CAS battery [Das & Naglieri, 1997] for assessment is also something different, although physically it looks like an usual test. The DN:CAS gives us a profile that is non-static but dynamic, that is, changeable. The neurological foundation for the PASS theory is being reinforced by the most recent functional magnetic resonance imaging (fMRI) studies [Cabeza & Nyberg, 2000; Van den Heuvel, 2005].

The emotional concept is far more elusive than the cognitive concept. In fact, what we see on reading the scientific literature is that emotion is cognitively explained. In other words, researchers study the cognition (thought) expressing feeling, which is not exactly feeling (sensitivity). A laudable effort for throwing light on the mental confusion has been brilliantly made some years ago [Power & Dalgleish, 1997].

In this line of thought, some concepts are crucial for our conception. One, the notion of reactive painful behaviors as a protective-defensive mechanism beyond any psychodynamic conceptualization [Lazarus, 1966; Horowitz, 1990]. Second, the meaning of the body language, which automatically-unconsciously express the feeling state of any person [Darwin, 1965; Ekman, 1973; Adolphs & Damasio, 2000; Adolphs et al., 2000], although body language can also convey informative cognitive content undoubtedly. And third, the proved evidence that verbal language incoherent with both body language and physiological reaction proves to be characteristic of the painful emotional-feeling behavioral response [Lang, 1984].

In defining the emotional concept we are dealing with, the scientific contributions from animal experimentation [LeDoux et al., 1984, 1986, 1990; LeDoux, 1995, 1996, 2000] have been substantial. What also may be considered relevant is some human clinical experience on emotional prefrontal [Damasio, 1994, 1995, 1999] and prefrontal - limbic system interaction [Goldberg, 2001]. We must insist the human fMRI investigation [Cabeza & Nyberg, 2000] proves to be concordant with the human clinical research.

INFORMATION PROCESSING

In chapter three we focus on the information processing phenomenon. We say that every processing is a mental activity independent of input and output of information, although visual input tends to be processed simultaneously and auditive input successively. Input and output, either verbal or manipulative, may be both successive and simultaneous, but both input and output may be successive and, instead, central processing simultaneous.

Neurological information processing runs a serial network between the input and output. Between the input and output, we can find different circuits from less to higher complexity. The more central, the more complex [Mesulan, 1998].The more complex, the less concentration of neurons. The PASS circuits must be considered highly complex.

The previous principle has been proved and reinforced by using different methodological studies like fMRI [Raichle, 1998; Cabeza & Nyberg, 2000], sound processing [Tallal, 1980: Tallal et al.,1993].

The practical importance of this notion is that we can successfully intervene, for instance, on a dyslexic problem [Das, 1998; Das et al. 1994,1996, 2000; Perez-Alvarez & Timoneda-Gallart, 2000] without using reading as a training material because reading is a behavioral output but not the mechanism of production. Likewise, we can treat attention deficit hyperactive disorder without dealing with either the inattentive or hyperactive behavior [Perez-Alvarez & Timoneda-Gallart, 1999c, 2001, 2004b].

According to PASS conceptualization, we can assess the PASS programs using the DN:CAS. The result is a current profile, but not necessarily the potential possible profile (dynamic concept of intelligence). The achieved profile can be changed for better by training the PASS planning, and inductively learning new principles, strategies, and beliefs (knowledge and feeling). Next, a comparison between DN:CAS and other usual tests is carried out to demonstrate how the DN:CAS has nothing to do with other classic batteries in terms of validity and reliability.

A particular comment is devoted to planning and attention because the usual concept of executive function does not distinguish between these two processes, which are usually put together under the same entity. Then, it is explained how memory is understood in the light of PASS theory.

A very important point is language processing and logic [Balmes, 1964; Shand, 2000] to understand how they both work under the influence of feeling processing. We can assert that emotion reactions are perfectly reasonable, and we are purely logical creatures. Likewise, understanding language processing and logic, we will be able to see how the beliefs are built.

The language produced under the painful feeling processing suffers from failure in good logical reasoning that can be verified in (a) contradiction between verbal language and body language, (b) contradiction in arguments of verbal language, if only in causal reasons argued, (c) disproportional cause-effect relationship susceptible to be seen in overacting verbal or/and body behavior (exaggerating-overreacting-disproportional behavior for the causal-effect reason either explicitly or implicitly argued), and (d) cognitive PASS planning dysfunction.

Apart from linguistic language, a human being also expresses himself with body language. Bodies talk, just as words do. For our procedure, body language interpretation is a basic mastering. Body language, including para-verbal language, conveys feeling apart from concepts.

Next, we devote the following paragraphs to discuss the foundation of learning from our point of view. Learning leads to knowledge base and beliefs. Before proceeding with other notions, we clarify how we understand the information neurological processing of beliefs (Das, 1999; Das et al., 1994, 1996, 2000; Perez-Alvarez & Timoneda, 2004). We emphasize that the PASS processes operate at a central level between input and output, as well as the beliefs likewise work at a central level between input and output. Therefore, evaluation (diagnosis) that exclusively examines the resulting product is not accurate.

We remark that the central-neurological processing happens more frequently unconsciously than consciously between the either consciously or unconsciously processed sensorial input (stimulus) and the either consciously or unconsciously processed output (response). This way, we introduce the notion of conscious versus unconscious processing, which is another basic concept for our procedure.

A considerable number of instances are analyzed to differentiate input from output, and from central processing. Knowledge base, beliefs, principles, rules, values all operate at central level. The focus is also put on conscious and unconscious processing.

In the following paragraphs we deal with the foundation of diagnosis and treatment. A successful treatment demands a precise diagnosis. Diagnosis and treatment implies learning, and particularly learning of beliefs, principles, rules, and knowledge definitely. This is applicable to both a learning dysfunction and a behavioral dysfunction. Essentially, the procedure consists of applying planning training. Planning training is not repetition, but inductive learning to produce not only near transfer but also far transfer. A number of examples are shown to see how these notions are applicable in practice.

We put an end to the previous line of thought postulating that the highest efficiency of any cognitive training depends more on neuronal network processing feeling than on neuronal network processing cognition. That is, the higher amelioration in cognitive performance after cognitive training may be mainly the consequence of the amelioration in feeling processing.

The chapter ends by making a comment on the cognitive-feeling interaction and particularly planning-feeling interaction, which provides us with a link to the next chapter on cognition and emotion. The emphasis is put on the notion of personal identity according to our conceptualization.

COGNITION AND EMOTION

In chapter four, we explain painful feeling processing in the light of neuroscience. First, we begin bringing up the relevant studies on fear processing [LeDoux et al., 1984, 1986, 1990; LeDoux, 1995, 1996, 2000]. We affirm that even though assuming the limitations inherent to an animal experiment and its extrapolation to human functioning, there is no reason, beyond any speculation, to think that the human cortex works in a different way. This evidence is a proof of the functional connection between the feeling processing and the cognitive processing.

Since the experience of interhemispheric disconnection, we can assert that the cognitive and feeling processing, although interconnected, could be dissociated [Gazzaniga & LeDoux, 1978; Sperry, 1983]. We had evidence that some kind of interhemispheric communication non-linked to the corpus callosum occurred. This intercommunication between one hemisphere and the other flows through deep areas of the brain in the absence of other connections. Anatomic-physiologic studies have reinforced this knowledge [Guyton & Hall, 1996]. This deep intercommunication is unconsciously processed.

We must remark that fMRI studies have demonstrated conscious-deliberate processing activates cortical areas whereas unconscious-automatic processing activates sub-cortical areas [Ojermann, 1976; Andreasen et al. 1995a, 1995b; Buckner et al. 1995; Tulving et al. 1996; Cabeza et al.1997; Jonides et al, 1998a, 1998b; Posner & Raichle, 1998; Smith et al, 1998; Cohen et al, 1999; Dolan & Fletcher, 1999; Dobbins et al., 2004; Sahrot et al. 2004]. Likewise, PET studies have revealed that a repetition task (priming) makes external cortical cerebral areas become less active (power cut) [Schacter et al. 1995; Blaxton et al. 1996; Schreurs et al. 1997].

The relevant fact is that the brain is able to switch from one modality to the other. Particularly, a recent fMRI study consisting of presenting different faces with different emotional expressions to a blind individual showed that emotional expressions were identified, but faces not, which occurred with amygdala activation [Sahrot et al. 2004]. In any case, we count on fMRI evidence that impicit learning activates the posterior brain, namely, parietal and occipital lobes, but not the anterior brain, that is, prefrontal lobe [Rauch et al. 1997; Deckersbach et al. 2002].

Concerning feeling, it is relevant that emotional stress may be associated with *theta* recording on EEG [Guyton & Hall, 1996], which is compatible with circumvention of the higher brain regions. Remember that this shortcut is equivalent to unconscious processing.

What is highly relevant is the conclusion that our brains might cheat when learning or behaving, switching to 'automatic pilot' mode whenever possible. Instead of trying to answer a question by reasoning, our brain explores a catalog of previous answers to similar questions. The brain builds a repertoire of rote responses to frequently encountered problems that it can use as appropriate. This cheating mechanism also exists in people suffering from amnesia. This mechanism is highly efficient whether it is about learning or non-learning [Dobbins et al., 2004].

Extrapolating animal experimentation [LeDoux et al., 1984, 1986, 1990; LeDoux, 1995, 1996, 2000] to the human brain functioning, we can neurologically explain that the cognitively thinking production of the cortex, operating under the order of the amygdala, is aimed not to stop the plan put into action when faced with a life-threatening condition. The cortex starts working and, as "a posteriori" action, it produces thinking that elaborates after processing the information entering the central nervous system coming from the external environment. When thinking activity happens, the thought produced is oriented to in real time explain or justify what that person can see, hear, touch, smell, and so on in the external scenery.

That's why logically there is contradiction between arguments due to "a posteriori" neocortical information processing and body language expression due to amygdalar feeling processing. Cerebral neocortex does not receive cognitive informative data from the amygdala, but a physiological signal to be codified as a danger, which demands some kind of action. Depending on the magnitude of the painful-emotional sensitivity processed by the amygdala, related to both the memorized painful-emotional experiences in the past (identity) and the precipitating (triggering) experiences in the present (current precipitant factors), the painful feeling sensation will vary from the unconscious to the conscious level. In any case, body language will convey a painful feeling sensation.

The previous arguments summarize how what we call masked behaviors happen as a consequence of painful feeling processing. Now, we raise a critical point. A brain operating in masked program makes masked decisions. We'll go over the most relevant aspects.

One of our princeps points is that the decision-making (act of will) is determined by feeling, but not really rational thinking. More exactly, it is determined by feeling associated with thought or cognitive data content processed. Studies based on neurological lesions have been substantial [Damasio 1994, 1995, 1999] for this conclusion. The determinant reason for behavior seems to be feeling, but not knowledge. For instance, any normal person behaves according to educational norms, it is said, because he/she has learnt (cognitive process) the norms, but clinical evidence of patients suffering from feeling-emotional prefrontal lesion (Damasio, 1994, 1995, 1999; Goldberg, 2001; Camille, 2004; Bechara, 2004) says otherwise. These patients behave against the educational norms because they do not feel badly, even though they rationally understand what they are doing. The experience with gambling points to the same conclusion [Bechara et al. 1997, 2005]. That is, an individual with a lesion in feeling medial-ventral-inferior prefrontal cortex, dorsolateral cortex being intact, behaves unsociably without remorse or, likewise, gamble without concern for the painful consequences [Damasio, 1994, 1995, 1999; Perez-Alvarez & Timoneda, 2005].

The experiment of Benjamin Libet, neurophysiologist of California University, after the previous studies of German neurophysiologist HH Kornhuber and L Decke is really astonishing [Degen, 2000, 2001; Libet, 1966, 1982]. From this, we can assume that a period of unconscious processing occur before a decision is made. Which kind of information is processed? Is it possible our brain unconsciously checks the memorized pool of our beliefs before making a decision?

In the same astonishing line, we count on evidence that skin conductance activity precede decision-making act [Bechara & Damasio, 1997; Bechara et al. 1997, 1999, 2000, 2005], which allows us to deduce that some kind of unconscious processing associated with somatic-visceral activity takes place before conscious decision-making happens. If so, we can assume that this previous unconscious processing influences our conscious-declarative decision-making. Strikingly, the more painful consequence follows decision-making, the more intense is the skin conductance activity [Bechara, 2004; Bechara & Damasio, 1997; Bechara et al. 1997; 1999; 2000, 2005]. Therefore, we can assert that an unconscious feeling processing precedes decision making. Is it linked to unconscious belief processing?

In sum, human clinical neurological evidence [Teuber, 1964; Luria, 1980; Stuss & Benson, 1986; Fuster, 1989; Thatcher, 1991, 1992] tells us that, indeed, planning [Das et al. 1996] depends on the prefrontal cortex. Since lesion studies, [Damasio, 1994, 1995, 1999], it was stated that two dissociable prefrontal cortex could be differentiated-dissociated, namely, the external cognitive dorsolateral prefrontal cortex and the medial-ventral-inferior "emotional" prefrontal cortex in charge of processing the feeling-sensitivity of the data (informative cognitive content). Finally, we have seen this evidence is convergent with the evidence reported by fMRI studies [Greene et al. 2001; Singer et al, 2004; Camille et al. 2004; Bechara, 2004; Perez-Alvarez et al. 2006c].

We must say that our fMRI study on decision making is extraordinarily revealing. In terms of neurological circuits, we can summarize that the recent evidence in animals together with old anatomical evidence and recent fMRI evidence in humans increasingly suggest that the painful feeling processing, in general, is supported by a network integrated by thalamus, amygdala, anterior and posterior cingulate cortex, insula, and anterior-ventral-medial prefrontal cortex, whereas the most external cortical structures, namely, dorsolateral prefrontal, temporal, parietal and occipital are responsible for the processing of concepts or ideas [Perez-Alvarez et al.2006b].

According to observational behavioral experience, the interaction cognition, in particular planning, and feeling is universally accepted. The clinical neurology [Goldberg, 2001] has provided us with evidence enough to support that a dysfunction in planning produces painful feeling and vice versa.

The following lines of our discussion have been devoted to exemplifying masked behaviors. We describe the behavior and explain it in the light of our framework, resorting to metaphors and practical examples. Perhaps, we must insist on the concept of conscious pleasant compensating feeling associated to behavior to compensate for unconscious painful-emotional feeling (lack of self-confidence), which is neurologically processed-codified as a danger signal. We must recall that the pleasure of a pleasant compensating behavior is not that of a non-compensating behavior. This last one is like tranquility, relaxation, happiness, and peace we can see in body language. As we have said, the personal unconfident feeling can be to a certain extent compensated for by means of compensating masked behaviors, but just to a certain extent.

The rest of the chapter is devoted to concisely discussing autism as a clinical model of our conception, our concept of impulsivity, the resistance and treatment, and finally the hypnosis.

OUR RESEARCH

In this chapter we summarize our scientific production in the field of cognition and emotion. We have diagnosed and treated cognitive and emotional problems, but we must say this dichotomy does not exist.

Cognitively, we have worked with the DN:CAS as an assessment battery. To start with, we, first of all, translated and validated it. Doing it, we were aware that an accurate observance of the norms is needed to reliably administer attention tests. Otherwise, attention tests measure planning.

Dyslexia has been a preferential focus of our research. We have diagnosed and treated dyslexic children according to the procedure we have described. We are very satisfied. Dyslexia is an example of the false dichotomy we have referred to.

In the field of behavioral dysfunction, attention deficit hyperactive disorder has been also one of our preferential dedications. ADHD is also another example of the false dichotomy.

However, the reader will have observed the enormous variety of dysfunctional behavior that we have diagnosed and treated. The procedure we use is based on the mechanism of production of behaviors. We diagnose etiopathogenesis and treat etiopathogenesis, but not signs or symptoms. Neurobiologically speaking, the mechanism we are talking about is present in every behavior.

We are particularly satisfied with our fMRI study where we demonstrate, beyond any reasonable limitation, that human decision making depends on feeling, but not reason, when enough painful feeling is present.

GUIDELINE

As we have already said, we are used to tons of theory and little practicality. Every day we confront theoretical discussions that lead nowhere. It is about the real nuts and bolts of teaching and helping children and persons in general. The study of how things work, on the idea that even the best you can find can probably be improved and/or combined with more of the best from somewhere else.

This chapter is above all practical. We have described the diagnosis and treatment beyond the cognitive assessment (psychometry).

Along the discussion, to conclude, we have tried to argue how human behavior can be explained according to what nowadays the CNS tell us about both the processing of cognitive information and the processing of the painful sensitivity. Even though certain deductions can be considered to be based on rather indirect demonstration with questionable demonstrative power, however the conclusions deserve to be considered beyond any speculation.

Whether or not you are persuaded by the arguments we have expressed, we hope you may at least reconsider some of your own assumptions about human behavior and the role of cognition and emotion, and their psychological assessment. The procedure we have discussed is useful for special populations, that is, disadvantaged children, learning disabled, mentally handicapped, special education children, slow learners, low achievers, environmentally deprived, brain-injured, gifted and handicapped children, socially and emotionally disturbed, etc. Remember, these general labels may be prejudicial, giving the impression that the child cannot be helped.

ACKNOWLEDGEMENTS

We are indebted to J Alabau, J Baus, J Hernández, S Mayoral, for his professional dedication, the children, and their parents for their invaluable collaboration.

This work was supported in part by the grants of the University of Girona (Spain) 265/1995; 181/1997; 393/1998-1999.

REFERENCES

Adolphs, R. & Damasio, A.R. (2000). Neurobiology of emotion at a systems level. In JC. Borod (Ed.), *The Neuropsychology of Emotion.* (pp. 194-213. Oxford: Oxford University Press.

Adolphs RH, Damasio D, Tranel G, Cooper A, Damasio AR. (2000). A role for somatosensory cortices in the visual recognition of emotion as revealed by 3 – 0 lesion mapping. *Journal Neuroscience, 20,* 2683-2690.

Alabau-Bofill J. (2003). Estudi dels processos emocionals en nens/nes amb dificultats d'aprenentatge i la seva relació amb els processos cognitius basats en la teoria PASS de la inteligel.lència [tesi doctoral]. Universitat de Girona. Gir

Amen DG & Carmichael BD. (1997). High-resolution brain SPECT imaging in ADHD. *Ann Clin Psychiatry, 9*: 81-86.

Andreasen NC, O'Leary DS, Amdt S, Cizallo T, Rezai K, Watkins GL, Porto LL, Hichwa RD.(1995a). I. PET studies of memory: novel and practiced free recall of complex narratives. *Neuroimage, 2,* 284-95.

Andreasen NC, O'Leary DS, Cizallo T, Amdt S, Rezai K, Watkins GL, Porto LL, Hichwa RD.(1995b). II. PET studies of memory: novel versus practiced free recall of word lists. *Neuroimage, 2,* 296-305.

Baddeley AD & Hitch GJ. (1974). Working Memory. In Bower GA (Ed.), *Recent advances in learning and motivation. Vol.8.* pp. 47-90. New York: Academic Press.

Balmes J. (1968). *El criterio.* Barcelona: Círculo de Lectores.

Bandura A. (1969). *Principles of behavior modification.* New York: Holt Rinehart Winston, Inc.

Barkley RA. (1997). Behavioral inhibition, sustained attention and executive functions: constructing a unifying theory of ADHD. *Psychol Bull, 21*: 65-94.

Barkley RA. (1998). *Attention Deficit Hyperactive Disorder. A handbook for diagnosis and treatment.*(2nd ed.). New York: Guilford Press.

Bateson G. (1979). *Mind and Nature: A necessary Unity.* New York: EP Dutton.

Bechara A. (2004). The role of emotion in decision-making: Evidence from neurological patients with orbitofrontal damage. *Brain Cogn, 55,* 30-40.

Bechara A & Damasio H. (1997). Deciding advantageously before knowing the advantageous strategy. *Science, 275,* 1293-5.

Bechara A, Tranel D, Damasio H. (2000). Characterization of the decision-making effect of patients with ventromedial prefrontal cortex lesions. *Brain, 123,* 2189-2202.

Bechara A, Damasio H, Tranel D, Damasio AR. (1997). Deciding advantageously before knowing the advantageous strategy. *Science, 275,* 1293-5.

Bechara A, Damasio H, Damasio AR, Lee SW. (1999). Different contributions of the human amygdala and ventromedial prefrontal cortex to decision making. *J Neurosci, 19,*5473-81.

Bechara A, Damasio H, Tranel D, Damasio AR. (2005).The Iowa Gambling Task and the somatic marker hypothesis: some questions and answers. *Trends Cogn Sci, 9,* 159-62.

Bhüler K. (1907) Tatsachen und probleme zu einer psychologie des denkvorgange. *Archiv für die Gesamte Psychologie, 9,* 297-305.

Blaxton TA, Zeffiro TA, Gabrieli JDE, Bookheimer SY, Carrillo MC, Theodore WH.(1996). Functional mapping of human learning: a positron emission tomography activation study of eyeblink condiitoning. *J Neurosci 16,* 4032-40.

Bolles RC. (1975a). *Learning theory.* New York: Holt.

Bolles RC. (1975b). Learning, motivation, and cognition. In Estes WK. (Ed.), *Handbook of learning and cognitive processes. Vol.1.* Hillsdale, NJ: Lawrence Erlbaum.

Bremmer JD, Randall T, Scott TM, Brunen RA, Seibyl JP, Southwick SM, Delaney RC, McCarthy G, Johnson CR, Charney DS, Innis RB. (1995). MRI-based measurement of hippocampal volume in patients with combat-related posttraumatic stress disorder. *American J Psychiatry, 152,* 973-981.

Bruner JS. (1966). *Toward a theory of instruction.* Cambridge: Belknap Press of Harvard University Press.

Buchsbaum MS. (1982). Role of opioid peptides in disorders of attention in psychopathology. *Proceedings New York Academy Science, 82,* 352-365.

Buckner RL, Raichle ME, Petersen SE. (1995). Dissociation of human prefrontal cortical areas across different speech production tasks and gender groups. *J Neurophysiol. 74,* 2163-73.

Cabeza R & Nyberg L. (2000). Imaging cognition II: an empirical review of 275 PET and fMRI studies. *J Cogn Neurosc, 12,* 1-47.

Cabeza R, Mangels J, Nyberg L, Habib R, Houle S, McIntosh AR, Tulving E. (1997). Brain regions differentially involved in remembering what and when: a PET study. *Neuron, 19,* 863-70.

Camille N, Coricelli G, Sallet J, Pradat-Diehl P, Duhamel JR, Sirigu A.(2004). The involvement of the orbitofrontal cortex in the experience of regret. *Science, 304,* 1167-1170.

Caplan D. (1992). *Language, Structure, Processing, and Disorders.* Cambridge, MA: Bradford MIT Press.

Chomsky N. (1986). *Knowledge of language.* MIT Press.

Churland PM (1989). A neurocomputational perspective. The nature of mind and the structure of the science. Cambridge, MA: MIT Press.

Cohen PF, Sossi V, Johnson RR, Ruth T. (1999). PET in Canada. Historical Perspectives, Current Status, Challenges to Future Growth. *Clin Positron Imaging, 2,* 345.

Crabtree BF & Miller WL. (1992). *Doing qualitative research.* Newbury Park, CA: Sage Publications.

Creswell JW. (1994). *Research design. Qualitative and quantitative approaches.* Thousand Oaks, CA: Sage Publications.

Damasio AR.(1994). *Descartes'Error.* New York: Putnam.

Damasio AR. (1995). *Descartes' error: Emotion, reason and the brain*. London: Picador.

Damasio AR. (1999). *The feeling of what happens: Body and emotion in the making of consciousness*. San Diego: Harcourt.

Darwin C. (1965). *The expression of the emotions in man and animals*. Chicago: Chicago University Press.

Das J.P. (1998). *Dyslexia & Reading difficulties*. Edmonton, Canada: University of Alberta.

Das JP. (1999a). A neo-Lurian approach to assessment and remediation. *Neuropsychology Review, 9*, 107-115.

Das JP. (1999b). *PREP: PASS Reading Enhancement Program*. Deal, NY: Sarka Educational Resources.

Das JP.(2003). Theories of intelligence: Issues and applications. In G Goldstein & SR Beers (Eds.), *Comprehensive handbook of psychological assessment. Vol. I. Intellectual and neuropsychological assessment*. John Wiley & Sons, Inc.

Das JP & Naglieri JA. (1997). *Cognitive Assessment System*. Illinois: Riverside Publishing.

Das JP, Kirby JR, Jarman RF. (1979*). Simultaneous and successive cognitive processes*. New York: Academic Press.

Das JP, Naglieri JA, Kirby JR. (1994). *Assessment of cognitive processes. The PASS theory of intelligence*. Massachussets: Allyn & Bacon, Inc.

Das JP, Kar R, Parrila RK. (1996). *Cognitive planning. The psychological basis of intelligent behavior*. London: Sage Publications Ltd.

Das JP, Garrido MA, Gonzalez M, Timoneda C, Pérez-Álvarez F. (2000). *Dislexia y dificultades de lectura*. Barcelona: Paidós Editorial.

Deckersbach T, Savage CR, Curran T, Bohne A, Wilhelm S, Baer L, Jenike MA, Rauch SL. (2002). A study of parallel implicit and explicit information processing in patients with obsessive-compulsive disorder. *Am J Psychiatry.159*, 1780-1782.

Degen R. (2000). *Lexicon der Psycho-Irrtümer*. Eichborn AG, Frakfurt am Main.

Degen R. (2001).*Falacias de la psicología*. Barcelona. Ediciones Robinbook.

Dehaene S & Changeux JP. (1997). A hierarchical neuronal network for planning behavior. *Proc Natl Acad Sci USA, 94*, 13293-8.

Delacato CH. (1966). *Neurological organization and reading*. Springfield, IL:Charles C. Thomas.

Delgado JM, Ferrús A, Mora F, Rubia FJ. (1998). Manual de neurociencia. Madrid: Síntesis.

Delini-Stula A & Schiwy W. (1991). Prevención de las crisis de angustia con imipramina y clomipramina: bases farmacológicas y resumen de los hallazgos clínicos. In Kielhoz P. & Adams C. *Estados de angustia y ansiedad*. pp. 45. Barcelona: Espaxs SA.

DeLong GR. (1999). Autism: New data suggest a new hypothesis. *Neurology, 52*, 911-916.

Di Martino A & Castellanos FX.(2003). Functional neuroimaging of social cognition in pervasive developmental disorders: a brief review. *Ann N Y Acad Sci.,1008*, 256-60.

Dobbins IG, Schnyer DM, Verfaellie M, Schacter DL. (2004). Cortical activity reductions during repetition priming can result from rapid response learning. *Nature, 428*, 316-9.

Dolan RJ & Fletcher PF. (1999). Encoding and retrieval in human medial temporal lobes: an empirical investigation using functional magnetic resonance imaging (fMRI). *Hippocampus, 9*, 25-34.

DSM-IV (2000). Diagnostic and Statistical Manual of Mental Disorders. 4th. Ed. Washington, DC:AMA.

Ekman P. (1973). Cross-cultural studies of facial expression. In P Ekman (Ed.), *Darwin and facial expression: A century of research in review*. New York: Academic Press.

Erickson E. (1991). Childhood in society. New York: WW Norton.

Erickson MH & Rossi E. (1981). *Experiencing hypnosis: Therapeutic approaches to altered states*. New York: Irvington.

Feuerstein R.(1983). *Instrumental Enrichment*. Baltimore: University Park Press.

Flynn JR. (1984). The mean IQ of Americans: massive gains 1932 - 1978. *Psychol Bull, 95*, 29 - 51.

Frith CD & Frith U. (1999). Interacting minds: a biological basis. *Science, 286*, 1629-5.

Fu-Ming Zhou, Yong Liang, Ramiro Salas, Lifen Zhang, Mariella De Biasi, John A. Dani. (2005). Corelease of Dopamine and Serotonin from Striatal Dopamine Terminals. *Neuron, 46*, 1.

Fuster JM. (1989). *The prefrontal cortex*. New York: Raven Press.

Galaburda AM. (1993). Dyslexia and development: neurobiological aspects of extra-ordinary brains. Cambridge: Harvard University Press.

Gallagher M & Holland P. (1994). The amygdala complex. *Proceeding National Academy Sciences, USA, 91*, 771-776.

Gazzaniga MS & LeDoux JE. (1978). The Integrated Mind. New York: Plenum.

Gillberg C. (1983). Perceptual, motor and attentional deficits in seven-years-old children. Neurological screening aspects. *Acta Paediatr Scandinavica, 89*, 302-9.

Goldberg E. (2001). *The executive brain*. Oxford University Press.

Goldstein RZ, Volkow ND, Wang GJ, Fowler JS, Rajaram S. (2001). Addiction changes orbitofrontal gyrus function: involvement in response inhibition. *Neuroreport, 12*, 2595-9.

Goleman DP. (1986). *Vital Lies, Simple Truths: The Psychology of Self-Deception*. New York: Touchstone Books.

Green, J. & Britten, N. (1998). Qualitative research and evidence based medicine. *British Medical Journal 316*: 1230-1232.

Greene JD, Sommerville RB, Nystrom LE, Darley JM, Cohen JD. (2001). An fMRI investigation of emotional engagement in moral judgment. *Science 293*:2105-8.

Greenhalgh T & Taylor R. (1997). Paper that go beyond numbers (qualitative research). *Br M J, 315*, 740-3.

Grinder J, DeLozier J, Bandler R.(1978). *Patterns of the Hypnotic Techniques of Milton H Erickson: Vol.II*. Cupertino, CA: Meta Publications.

Guilford JP.(1980). Teorias de la inteligencia. In Wolman B. (Ed.), *Manual de psicología*. Barcelona: Martínez Roca.

Guyton AC. (1971). *Tratado de fisiología médica*. 4 ed. México: Interamericana.

Guyton AC & Hall JE.(1996). *Textbook of Medical Physiology*. (9th ed.) Philadelphia: W.B. Saunders Company.

Hebb DO. (1949). *The organization of behavior*. New York: John Wiley & Sons, Inc.

Hebb DO (1968). Concerning imagery. *Psychological Review, 75,*466-477.

Hollander E. (2001). New developments in impulsivit. *Lancet, 358*, 949-50.

Hollander E, Posner N, Cherkasky S.(2003). *The neuropsychiatry of aggression and impulse control disorders*. In Yudofsky SC & Hales RE. (Eds.), Washington DC: American Psychiatric Press, Inc.

Horowitz M.J. (1990). A model of mourning: Changes in schemas of self and others. *J American Psychoanalytic Association, 38,* 297-324.

Ionnidis JPA. (2005). Why most published research findings are false. *PlosMed, 2,* 696-701. DOI: 10.1371/journal.pmed 0020124

James W. (1890). *The principles of psychology.* New York: Holt.

Jones R. (1995). Why do qualitative research. *Br M J, 311,* 2.

Jonides J, Smith EE, Marshuetz C, Koeppe RA, Reuter-Lorenz PA. (1998a). Inhibition in verbal working memory revealed by brain activation. *Proc Natl Acad Sci U S A., 95,* 8410-3.

Jonides J, Schumacker EH, Smith EE, Koeppe RA, Awh E, Reuter-Lorentz PA, Marshuetz C, Willis CR. (1998b). The role of parietal cortex in verbal working memory. *J Neurosci.,18,* 5026-34.

Just MA & Carpenter PA. (1987). *The Psychology of Reading and Language Comprehension.* Boston, MA: Allyn & Bacon.

Kapp BS, Whalen PJ, Supple WF, Pascoe JP. (1992). Amygdaloid contribution to conditioned arousal and sensory information processing. In Aggleton JP. (Ed.), *The amygdala: Neurobiological aspects of emotion, memory, and mental dysfunction.* New York: Wiley - Liss.

Kintsch W. (1988). The role of knowledge in discourse comprehension: A construction integration model. *Psychological Review, 95,* 163-182.

Kohlberg L. (1992). *Psicología del desarrollo moral.* Bilbao: Desclée de Brouwer.

Lamote de Grignon. (1993). Barcelona: *Antropología neuroevolutiva. Un estudio sobre la naturaleza humana.* Barcelona: Faes Farma.

Lang PJ. (1984). Cognition in emotion. In Izard CE, Kagan J & Zajonc RB. (Eds.), *Emotions, cognition and behavior.* New York: Cambridge University Press.

Lazarus RS. (1966). *Psychological stress and the coping process.* New York: McGraw-Hill.

LeDoux JE. (1995).Emotion clues from the brain. *Annual Review Psychol, 46*:209-235.

LeDoux JE. (1996). *Emotional brain.* New York: Simon & Schuster.

LeDoux JE. (2000). Cognitive-emotional interactions. In Lane RD & Nadel L, (Eds.), *Cognitive neuroscience of emotion.* pp. 129-55. New York: Oxford UniversityPress.

LeDoux JE, Sakaguchi A, Reis DJ. (1984). Subcortical efferent projections from the medial geniculate nucleus mediate emotional responses conditioned by acoustic stimuli. *Journal Neuroscience, 4,* 683-698.

LeDoux JE, Farb CF, Ruggiero DA. (1990). Topographic organization of neurons in the acoustic thalamus that project to the amygdala. *Journal Neuroscience, 10,* 1043-1054.

LeDoux JE, Sakaguchi A, Iwata J, Reis DJ. (1986). Interruption of projections from the medial geniculate body to an archi-neostriatal field disrupts the classical conditioning of emotional responses to acoustic stimuli in the rat. *Neuroscience, 17,* 615-627.

Libet B. (1966). Brain stimulation and the threshold of conscious experience. In Eccles JC (Ed.), *Brain and conscious experience.* pp. 165-81.New York. Springer Verlag.

Libet B. (1982).Brain stimulation in the study of neuronal functions for conscious sensory experiences. *Human Neurobiology,1,* 235-42.

Luria AR. (1980). *Higher cortical functions in man.* New York: Basic Books.

Lyons W. (1980). *Emotion.* Cambridge UK: Cambridge University Press.

Madanes C. (1985). Finding a humorous alternative. In Zeig JK. (Ed.), *Ericksonian Psychotherapy. Vol. II: Clinical Applications.*pp. 24-43. New York: Brunner / Mazel.

Magarinos AM, McEwen BS, Flugge G, Fuchs E. (1996). Chronic psychosocial stress causes apical dendriticatrophy of hippocampal CA3 pyramidal neurons in subordinate tree shrews. *J Neuroscience, 16,* 3534 - 3540.

Matute E, Roselli M, Ardila A, Ostrosky-Solis F. (2005). Evaluación Neuropsicológica Infantil. Mexico: Manual Moderno. Universidad de Guadalajara.

Mayoral-Rodríguez S. (2002). Diagnòstic i intervenció en alumnes d'educació secundària amb problemes d'agressivitat: una proposta per a la millora de l'atenció psicopedagògica. [tesi doctoral]. Universitat de Girona.

Mays N & Pope C. (1995). Rigour and qualitative research. *Br M J, 311,* 109-12.

Mesulam MM. (1987). Asymmetry of neural feedback in the organization of behavioral states. *Science, 237,* 537-8.

Mesulam, MM. (1998). From sensation to cognition. *Brain, 121,* 1013-1052.

Mesulam, M.M. (2000). Behavioral neuroanatomy: large-scale networks, association cortex, frontal syndromes, the limbic system, and hemispheric specialization. In MM. Mesulam (Ed.), *Principles of Behavioral and Cognitive Neurology* (2nd ed.). pp. 1-120. Nueva York: Oxford University Press.

Minuchin S. (1974). *Families and Family Therapy.* Cambridge: Harvard University Press.

Molfese DL, Freeman RB, Palermo DS. (1975). The Ontogeny of the Brain Lateralization for Speech and Nonspeech Stimuli. *Brain and Language, 2,* 356-368.

Morgan MA, Romanski LM, LeDoux JE. (1993). Extinction of emotional learning: contribution of medial prefrontal cortex. *Neuroscience Letters, 163,* 109 - 113.

Narbona J & Chevrie-Muller C. (1996). *El lenguaje del niño.* Barcelona: Masson.

Nestler EJ. (2001).Molecular basis of long term plasticity underlying addiction. *Nat Rev Neurosci, 2, 119-28.*

Ojemann GA. (1976). Subcortical Language Mechanism. In Whitaker H & Whitaker HA. (Eds.), *Studies in Neurolinguistics. Vol.1.* New York: Academic Press.

Olpe HR & Schellenberg A. (1981). The sensitivity of cortical neurons to serotonin: effect of chronic treatment with antidepressants, serotonin-uptake inhibitors and monoamino-oxidase-blocking drugs. *J Neural Transmiss, 51,*233.

Patel RS, Bowman FD, Rilling JK. (2005).A Bayesian approach to determining connectivity of the human brain. *Hum Brain Mapp, 27,* 267-276.

Penfield W & Rasmussen T. (1957). *The Cerebral Cortex of Man: A Clinical Study of Localization of Functions.* New York: MacMillan Publishing.

Penfield W & Perot P. (1963). The brain's record of auditory and visual experience. *Brain, 86,* 595-696.

Pérez-Alvarez F & Timoneda C. (1996). Epilepsia y aprendizaje. *Rev Neurol, 24,* 825-8.

_____. (1998). *Neuropsicopedagogia. ¿Es como parece?.* Barcelona: Editorial Textos Universitarios Sant Jordi.

_____. (1999a). Cognición, emoción y conducta. *Rev Neurol, 29,* 26-33.

_____ (1999b). Fenotipos conductuales: Explicación cognitiva y emocional. *Rev Neurol, 29,* 1153-1159.

_____ (1999c). El hiperquinético a la luz del PASS. *Rev Neurol, 28,* 472-475.

_____ (1999d). El PASS y la disfasia, dislexia e hiperquinético. *Rev Neurol, 28* (Supl.), 193.

_____ (1999e). La disfasia y la dislexia a la luz del PASS. *Rev Neurol, 28,* 688-69.

_____(2000). Disfunción del procesamiento secuencial PASS en la dislexia. *Rev Neurol, 30,* 614-619. http://www.revneurol.com/3007/i070614.pdf.

_____. (2001). Disfunción neurocognitiva PASS del déficit de atención *Rev Neurol, 32*, 30-37. http://www.revneurol.com/3201/k010030.pdf

_____. (2002). Conductas emocionales como disfunción neurológica. *Rev Neurol, 35*, 612-624. http://www.revneurol.com/LinkOut/form MedLine.asp?Refer=2001110

_____.(2004a). Learning Both in Attention Deficit Disorder and Dyslexia in the light of PASS Neurocognitive Dysfunction. In HD Tobias (Ed.), *Focus on Dyslexia Research.* pp. 173-179. Hauppauge, NY: Nova Science Publishers, Inc.

_____.(2004b). Attention Deficit / Hyperactive Disorder as Impulsivity Disorder according to PASS Neurocognitive Function. In P. Larimer (Ed.), *Attention Deficit Hyperactivity Disorder Research Developments.* pp 173-184. Hauppauge, NY: Nova Science Publishers, Inc.

_____. (2005). La función intelectual: ¿De qué se trata? *Acta Pediatr Esp, 63*,101-4.

_____ (2006) Assessment of Cognitive Processes: The Basis of Intelligent Behavior. In F Columbus (Ed.), *Psychological Tests and Testing.* pp. Hauppage, NY: Nova Science Publishers, Inc. (in press).

Perez-Alvarez F, Timoneda C, Baus J. (2002). Topiramate monotherapy in children with newly diagnosed epilepsy. *Epilepsia,* (Supl. 8), 187.

Perez-Alvarez F, Timoneda C, Baus J.(2006a) Topiramato y epilepsia a la luz del Das-Naglieri Cognitive Assessment System. *Rev Neurol, 42*, 3-7.

Perez-Alvarez F, Timoneda C, Reixach J. (2006b). An fMRI study of emotional engagement in decision-making. *Transaction Advanced Research, 2*, 45-51.

Perez-Alvarez F, Luque A, Peñas A. (2006c). Bilateral disc drusen as an important differential diagnosis of pseudotumor cerebri. *Brain Development* (in press).

Pérez-Alvarez F., Timoneda C., Font X., Mayoral S. (1999). Inteligencia PASS y Síndrome de Williams. *Rev Neurol 28* (Supl.), 201.

Perez-Alvarez F, Peñas A, Bergada A, Mayol Ll. (2006d). Obsessive-compulsive disorder and acute traumatic brain. *Acta Psychiatr Scand, 114*, 295.

Perez-Alvarez F, Mayol Ll, Luque A, Peña A. (2006e). Pseudohypoparathyroidism, movement disorder, and non-organic disease. *J Neurol Neurosurg Ps.* URL: http://jnnp.bmjjournals.com/cgi/eletters/68/2/207

Petrides M. (1994). Frontal lobes and working memory: evidence from investigations of the effects of cortical excisions in nonhuman primates. In Boller F & Grafman J. (Eds.), *Handbook of neuropsychology.* pp. 59-82. Amsterdam: Elsevier.

Peyron R, Laurent B, García-Larrea L. (2000). Functional imaging of brain responses to pain. *Neurophysiol Clin, 30,*263-88.

Piaget J. (1964) Development and learning. In RE Ripple & VN Rockcastle (Eds.) *Piaget rediscovered.* Ithaca, NY: Cornell University.

Pinel JPJ. (2000). *Biopsychology.* (4th ed.). Allyn & Bacon.

Posner MI & Raichle ME. (1998). The neuroimaging of human brain function. *Proc Natl Acad Sci U S A., 95,* 763-4.

Power M & Dalgleish T. (1997). *Cognition and Emotion. From order to disorder.* UK: Psychology Press, Publishers.

Quirk GJ, Repa JC, LeDoux JE. (1995). Fear conditioning enhances auditory short-latency responses of single units in the lateral nucleus of the amygdala: Simultaneous multichannel recording in freely behaving rats. *Neuron, 15,* 1029 - 1039.

Raichle ME. (1998). Behind the scenes of functional brain imaging: A historical and physiological perspective. *Proc Natl Acad Sci, 95,* 765-772.

Rapin I & Allen DA. (1983). Developmental language disorders: nosologic considerations. In Kirt U (Ed.), *Neuropsychology of language, reading, and spelling.* New York: Academic Press.

Rapin I & Allen DA. (1988). *Syndromes in developmental dysphasia and adult aphasia.* In Plum F (Ed.), *Language, communication and the brain.* pp. 57. New York. Raven Press.

Rauch SL, Savage CR, Alpert NM, Dougherty D, Kendrick AD, Curran T, Brown, HD, Manzo P, Fischman AJ, Jenike MA. (1997). Probing striatal function in obsessivecompulsive disorder: a PET study of implicit sequence learning. *J Neuropsychiatry Clin Neurosci. 9,* 568-573.

Rogers C. (1959). A theory of therapy, personality, and interpersonal relationship, as developed in the client-centered framework. In Koch S. (Ed.), *Psychology: A study of a Science.* pp. 184-256. New York: McGraw-Hll.

Rogers C. Rogers K, Erickson MH. (1987). A personal perspective on some similarities and differenecs. In Zeig J.(Ed.), *The evolution of psychotherapy.* pp. 179-87. New York: Brunner / Mazel.

Ros S, Peris MD, Arranz J. (2002). Topiramato en el tratamiento de los trastornos de la impulsividad. *Psiaquiatría Biológica, 9* (Supl. 2): 1-5.

Schachter S & Singer JE. (1962). Cognitive, social, and physiological determinants of emotional state. *Psychological Review*, 69,379-399.

Schacter DL, Reiman E, Uecker A, Polster MR, Yun LS, Cooper LA. (1995). Brain regions associated with retrieval of structurally-coherent visual information. *Nature, 376,* 587-90.

Schreurs BG, McIntosh AR, Bahro M, Herscovitch P, Sunderland T, Molchan SE. (1997). Lateralization and behavioral correlation of changes in regional cerebral flow with classical conditioning of the human eyeblink response. *J Neurophysiol, 77,* 2153-63.

Selye H. (1974). *The Stress of My Life: A Scientist's Memoirs.* New York: Van Nostrand Reinhold.

Shallice T. (1988). *From neuropsychology to mental structure.* Cambridge: Cambridge University Press.

Shand J. (2000). *Arguing well.* New York: Routledge.

Sharot T, Delgado MR, Phelps A. (2004). How emotion enhances the feeling of remembering. *Nature Neuroscience, 7, 1376-80.*

Shaywitz BA, Fletcher JM, Shaywitz SE. (1995). Defining and classifying Learning Disabilities and Attention Deficit Hyperactive Disorder. *J Child Neurol, 10* (S 1), 50-7.

Shaywitz SE. (1998). Dyslexia. *N Engl J Med, 338,* 307-312.

Shumyatsky GP, Malleret G, Shin RM, Takizawa S, Tully K, Tsvetkov E, Zakharenko SS, Joseph J, Vronskaya S, Yin D, Schubart UK, Kandel ER, Bolshakov VY. (2005). Stathmin, a gene enriched in the amygdala, controls both learned and innate fear. *Cell, 123,* 697-709.

Singer T, Seymour B, O'Doherty J, Kaube H, Dolan RJ, Frith CD.(2004). Empathy for pain involves the affective but not sensory components of pain. *Science, 303,* 1157-1162.

Smith EE, Jonides J, Marshuetz C, Koeppe RA. (1998). Components of verbal working memory: evidence from neuroimaging. *Proc Natl Acad Sci U S A.,* 95, 876-82.

Sperry R. (1983). *Science and Moral Priority.* New York: Columbia University Press.

Springer SP, Deutsch G. (1988). *Cerebro izquierdo, cerebro derecho.* Madrid: Alianza.

Stevens B & Grunan RE. (2005). Pain in Vulnerable Infants. *Clinics in Perinatology*,29, 373-394.

Stuss DT & Benson DF. (1986). *The frontal lobes*. New York: Raven Press.

Sugarman LL.(1996). *Hypnosis: Teaching children self-regulation. Pediatr Review, 17,* 5-11.

Tallal P. (1980). Auditory temporal perception, phonics, and reading disabilities in children. *Brain Lang, 9,* 182-98.

Tallal P, Miller S, Fitch R. (1993). Neurobiological basis of speech: a case for the preeminence of temporal processing. *Ann NY Acad Sci, 682,* 27-47.

Teuber HL. (1964). The riddle of frontal lobe function in man. In Warren JM & Akert K. (Eds.), *The frontal granular cortex and behavior.* pp. 410-444. New York: Mc Graw-Hill.

Thatcher RW.(1991). Maturation of human frontal lobes: Physiological evidence for staging. *Developmental Psychology, 7,* 397-419.

_____. (1992). Cyclic cortical reorganization during early childhood. *Brain and Cognition,* 20,24-50.

Timoneda-Gallart C & Perez-Alvarez F. (1994). *Successive and simultaneous processing in preschool children.* pp.156. Madrid: Proceeding Book 23rd International Congress of Applied Psychology.

Tulving E, Markowitsch HJ, Craik FE, Habib R, Houle S. (1996). Novelty and familiarity activation in PET studies of memory encoding and retrieval. *Cereb Cortex.* 6, 71-9.

Van den Heuvel OA, Veltman DJ, Groenewegen HJ, Cath DC, Van Balkom AJLM, Van Hartskam J, Barkhof F, Van Dick R. (2005). Frontal-striatal Dysfunction During Planning in Obsessive Compulsive Disorder. *Arch Gen Psychiatry, 62,* 301-310.

Vilanova, JC, Pujol J, Barceló J, Llach S, Cicres J, Pérez-Álvarez, F.(2003). *Dynamic phonetic articulation assessment by gated MRI.* Holland: Proceeding Book 20th Annual Scientific Meeting – ESMRMB 2003.

Volkow ND, Fowler JS. (2000). Addiction, a disease of compulsion and drive: involvement of the prefrontal cortex. *Cereb Cortex, 10,* 318-25.

Vygotsky L. (1978). *Mind in society: The developmental of higher psychological processes.* Cambridge MA: Harvard University Press.

Watzlawick P. (1985). Hypnotherapy without trance. In Zeig JK. (Ed.), *Ericksonian Psychotherapy. Vol. I. Structures.* pp.210-233.New York: Brunner / Mazel.

Welsh MC & Pennninton BF. (1988). Assessing frontal lobe functioning in childern: Views from developmental psychology. *Developmental Neuropsychology, 4*:199-230.

Zametkin AJ, Nordahl TE, Gross M. (1990). Cerebral glucose metabolism in adults with hyperactivity of chilhood onset. *N Engl J Med, 323,* 1361-6.

INDEX

C

G

H

I